FREE TIME

FREE TIME

JULIE L. ROSE

PRINCETON UNIVERSITY PRESS
PRINCETON AND OXFORD

Published by Princeton University Press,
41 William Street, Princeton, New Jersey 08540
In the United Kingdom: Princeton University Press,
6 Oxford Street, Woodstock, Oxfordshire OX20 1TR

press.princeton.edu

ISBN 978-0-691-16345-1

Library of Congress Control Number: 2016944395

British Library Cataloging-in-Publication Data is available

This book has been composed in Sabon Next LT Pro

Printed on acid-free paper ∞

Printed in the United States of America

10 9 8 7 6 5 4 3 2 1

FOR MY FAMILY,
AND FOR HERSCHEL

CONTENTS

ACKNOWLEDGMENTS

I have benefited immensely from the support of many people and institutions while writing this book, and I am grateful to have the opportunity to acknowledge them here. While any remaining errors are my own, the book is much better for their generous help. The book began at Princeton University in the Department of Politics and Program in Political Philosophy, where I received the support of the University Center for Human Values. Charles Beitz has been a truly wonderful advisor from the inception of this project, and I am tremendously grateful to him for his clear-sightedness and wisdom, on matters great and small, throughout. Melissa Lane, a constant source of encouragement and support, immeasurably helped the project with her wide-ranging contributions and me with her generous mentorship. Alan Patten provided exceptionally incisive comments at each stage, and my argument, from its foundations to extensions, has been shaped to a remarkable degree by my attempts to meet his objections. Stephen Macedo served as an ideal examiner, and I am grateful for his insightful comments and generous support throughout and beyond this project. Philip Pettit provided excellent advice throughout, and especially in the important early stages.

I was fortunate to spend two postdoctoral years in the stimulating intellectual communities of Brown University's Political Theory Project and Stanford University's McCoy Family Center for Ethics in Society. I am especially grateful to John Tomasi, Debra Satz, and Rob Reich for their invaluable support and guidance. Dartmouth College has been the ideal place to revise and complete the manuscript, with welcoming and encouraging colleagues in the Government Department and friends in the Philosophy and Economics Departments.

Special thanks are due to those who read versions of the full manuscript. Lucas Stanczyk and Rob Reich provided careful and insightful comments as part of a book manuscript workshop generously sponsored by the John

Sloan Dickey Center for International Understanding at Dartmouth. Lucas Swaine, James Bernard Murphy, Michelle Clarke, Russell Muirhead, Sonu Bedi, and Ira Lindsay also provided immensely helpful comments and conversations as part of, and beyond, the workshop. John Tomasi and, at his generous insistence, the excellent students in our Labor and Leisure graduate seminar at Brown provided encouraging comments on an early draft.

Many more people than I can list have contributed to this book with illuminating comments, questions, and conversations. I am especially grateful to Samuel Arnold, Michael Bittman, Brookes Brown, Robert Goodin, Alex Gourevitch, Alex Levitov, Eric MacGilvray, Kristi Olson, Jakob Reckhenrich, Liam Shields, Seana Valentine Shiffrin, Jeff Spinner-Halev, Anna Stilz, and James Lindley Wilson for providing comments on portions of the manuscript, and to Douglas Bamford, Eric Beerbohm, Michal Ben Noah, Brian Berkey, Corey Brettschneider, Thomas Christiano, Sarah Cotterill, Alexander Duff, David Estlund, Stephen Galoob, Javier Hidalgo, Dana Howard, Brian Hutler, Benjamin McKean, James Morone, Sara Mrsny, Jennifer Nedelsky, Anne Newman, Martin O'Neill, Thomas Parr, Govind Persad, Georg Picot, Jeppe von Platz, Jonathan Quong, Christian Schemmel, Laurie Shrage, Hillel Steiner, Timothy Syme, and Liza Williams for particularly helpful exchanges. I am also grateful to Mark Budolfson, Jorah Dannenberg, Ryan Davis, Loubna El Amine, Sandra Field, Jessica Flanigan, Jeffrey Friedman, Paul Frymer, Sarah Goff, Burke Hendrix, Keith Hernandez, Yonatan Herzbrun, Amy Hondo, Rob Hunter, Trevor Latimer, Marialanna Lee, Lida Maxwell, Matthew McCoy, Alison McQueen, Evan Oxman, Mariah Pfeiffer, Chris Ro, Genevieve Rousseliere, Tamar Schapiro, Kathryn Schwartz, Neil Shenai, Claire Shields, Patrick Taylor Smith, Hillel Soifer, Lauri Tähtinen, Philip Wallach, Oscar Westesson, Casey Williams, and Thomas Youle for their conversation, support, and friendship.

I have been fortunate to present portions of the book at various points to audiences at Princeton University, Harvard University, Brown University, Stanford University, Dartmouth College, the University of Manchester, the University of California, Los Angeles, Massachusetts Institute of Technology, the University of Pennsylvania, and Texas Christian University, as well as at meetings of the American Political Science Association, New England Political Science Association, Law & Society Association, Western Political Science Association, and Midwest Political Science Association. The comments and questions from these audiences were tremendously helpful.

Chapter 4 is a revised and extended version of "Money Does Not Guarantee Time: Discretionary Time as a Distinct Object of Distributive Justice,"

Journal of Political Philosophy 22 (2014): 438–57, and Chapter 5 was previously published as "Freedom of Association and the Temporal Coordination Problem," *Journal of Political Philosophy* 24 (2016): 261–76.

I am very grateful to Rob Tempio for his encouraging support of this book from an early stage and his patient shepherding since, to those with Princeton University Press who had a hand in bringing this project to completion, especially Joseph Dahm, Ryan Mulligan, and Jenny Wolkowicki, and to the Press's reviewers for their insightful and constructive comments.

I am also thankful to my undergraduate professors at Cornell University, Nick Salvatore, Isaac Kramnick, George Boyer, and Michael Gold, for showing me the quiet joys of an academic life, and giving me the confidence to pursue it for myself.

I am profoundly grateful to my family—to my grandparents, Sarah La-Shomb, Marguerite Rose, and Pete Rose, and my extended Rose, LaShomb, Moskow, and Freedman-Weiss families—for their love and wisdom and for being a reminder of what really matters. Most especially, my parents, Susan and Michael Rose, and my brother, Phil Rose, have been a constant source of unconditional support, and my parents' dedication, sacrifices, and values have, in many ways, inspired this project and my work.

Finally, my deepest debt of gratitude is to Herschel Nachlis, who has contributed to this book more than anyone, by sharing his advice on all points, providing unwavering support, and bringing me incredible happiness.

FREE TIME

CHAPTER I

INTRODUCTION

I.I HOURS FOR WHAT WE WILL

Many people, including in the contemporary United States, have little free time. They must spend long hours in paid work, household labor, personal care, and caregiving. They have little time to devote to any ends beyond meeting the necessities of life. This book argues that in the just society all citizens would have their fair shares of free time, time they could devote to the pursuit of their own projects and commitments.

As a matter of liberal egalitarian justice, all citizens are entitled to a fair share of free time—time not consumed by meeting the necessities of life, time that one can devote to one's chosen ends. Free time is a resource that citizens generally require to pursue their conceptions of the good, whatever those may be. Without the resource of free time, citizens lack the means to exercise their formal liberties and opportunities. In order to ensure that citizens can exercise their freedoms, a central commitment of liberal egalitarian theories of justice, citizens must be guaranteed their fair shares of free time.

This argument is absent from contemporary political philosophy, but it can be found in the origins of liberal egalitarian ideas, among nineteenth-century labor reformers. Early American journeymen argued that they had a "just right" to the time necessary to exercise their political liberties. In order to exercise their rights as enfranchised citizens, they argued that they required free time to acquire information and study the interests of their country. Unrelenting work diminished the value of their liberties, as it rendered

1

"the benefits of our liberal institutions to us inaccessible and useless."[1] Over the course of the nineteenth century, as labor's call went from ten hours of work to eight hours with a day of rest, workers drew on this argument more broadly to claim time to exercise their full set of liberties, for education, family, association, and religion.[2] As trade union leader William Sylvis argued, "It is true that churches are erected, school houses are built, mechanics' institutes are founded and libraries ready to receive us . . . but alas! We lack *the time to use them*—time."[3] To enjoy their rights to "life, liberty, and the pursuit of happiness," they must have the "*means*" to make use of them.[4] The final extension of this line of argument was that workers were entitled to free time not only for the exercise of a set of specific and fundamental liberties, but to do anything they wished. Workers argued that they were entitled to "eight hours for work, eight hours for rest, and eight hours for what we will."[5]

This book defends that idea: we have a just claim to "hours for what we will." Citizens are entitled to time that is not consumed by meeting the necessities of life, so they can have time to devote to any other pursuits they might choose—whether familial, religious, associational, recreational, political, creative, productive, or of any other sort. They are entitled to time to find and follow their own projects and commitments. They are entitled to a fair share of free time.

---

1 "Journeymen Carpenters' Ten-Hour Demand," *Democratic Press*, June 14, 1827, and "Preamble of the Mechanics' Union of Trade Associations," *Mechanics' Free Press*, April 19, 1828, quoted in David R. Roediger and Philip S. Foner, *Our Own Time: A History of American Labor and the Working Day* (London: Verso, 1989), 14, 15.

2 See Alex Gourevitch, *From Slavery to the Cooperative Commonwealth: Labor and Republican Liberty in the Nineteenth Century* (New York: Cambridge University Press, 2015), 126–32, 144–45.

3 William Sylvis, "Address Delivered at Boston, January 1867," in *The Life, Speeches, Labors and Essays of William H. Sylvis*, ed. James C. Sylvis (1872; repr., New York: Augustus M. Kelley, 1968), 199, emphasis original, quoted in Roediger and Foner, *Our Own Time*, 99.

4 "The Working Men's Declaration of Independence," December 1829, in *We, the Other People*, ed. Philip S. Foner (Urbana: University of Illinois Press, 1976), 49, emphasis original. The claim that citizens are entitled to the means to exercise their freedoms is regularly repeated in labor's alternative declarations.

5 Roy Rosenzweig, *Eight Hours for What We Will: Workers and Leisure in an Industrial City, 1870–1920* (Cambridge: Cambridge University Press, 1983). See also Benjamin Kline Hunnicutt, *Free Time: The Forgotten American Dream* (Philadelphia: Temple University Press, 2013), 1–94.

I.2 THE CLAIM TO FREE TIME

Contemporary liberal egalitarian theories of justice have given little attention to the demand for more "hours for what we will." They have instead implicitly assumed that how much leisure time citizens have is not an appropriate concern of a liberal theory of justice. They have understood leisure to be part, to varying extents, of some ideas of the good life, and not a part of others. Because it is not the proper role of a politically liberal state to promote some conceptions of the good life over others, it is presumptively impermissible for the state to act with the aim of providing or promoting leisure time.[6]

Instead, in accordance with the standard liberal egalitarian approach to distributive justice, *liberal proceduralism*, it is held that so long as just background conditions—that is, a just distribution of liberties, opportunities, and resources like income and wealth—obtain, citizens can choose their leisure patterns based on their own ideas of the good life, and whatever distribution of leisure results is presumptively just. Some citizens will want to work long hours and have little leisure, while others will want to work few hours and have more leisure. The resulting distribution of leisure will be unequal, true, but on this approach that in itself is not a cause for concern. On the contrary, for the state to aim at some particular distribution of leisure, absent some special justification, would be objectionable, for it would be impermissibly paternalistic, perfectionist, or otherwise partial to one conception of the good over another. Instead of attending to the distribution of leisure, the state should ensure that just background conditions under which citizens can fairly choose to pursue work or leisure, obtain.

The liberal proceduralist approach to distributive justice is to ensure that all citizens have fair access to *specific goods*, the particular components of one's particular conception of the good, by ensuring a fair distribution of *resources*, the all-purpose means that are generally required to pursue any conception of

6 Political theorists writing in other traditions have devoted greater attention to leisure time. For recent approaches from the Marxist and feminist traditions, see Nichole Marie Shippen, *Decolonizing Time: Work, Leisure, and Freedom* (New York: Palgrave Macmillan, 2014) and Kathi Weeks, *The Problem with Work: Feminism, Marxism, Antiwork Politics, and Postwork Imaginaries* (Durham, NC: Duke University Press, 2011). These issues have also received attention in the popular press, including the recent contribution of Brigid Schulte, *Overwhelmed: How to Work, Love, and Play When No One Has the Time* (New York: Farrar, Straus, and Giroux, 2014). The current discussion and awareness is heavily indebted to Juliet B. Schor's *The Overworked American: The Unexpected Decline of Leisure* (New York: Basic Books, 1992).

the good. Leisure has been understood, on the basis of both its philosophical and economic treatments, as a specific good. Leisure is variously defined as time engaged in intrinsically valuable activities, or as time in play and recreation, or as time not engaged in paid work, and on each understanding, as a specific good.

This narrow understanding of leisure time is, however, incomplete. Though "leisure" does correspond to goods that are appropriately regarded as specific goods (contemplation, play, time not working), it also refers to an idea that is best understood as a resource. This is the idea that the slogan "hours for what we will" captures—it is the time one can spend at one's discretion, pursuing one's own ends. It is, in a word, *free* time. Citizens require such time—time not committed to meeting the necessities of life—to pursue their conceptions of the good, whatever those may be.

When one redescribes the specific good of leisure as the resource of free time, the liberal's neglect of time loses its foundation. If free time is a resource, then its just distribution is no longer something that *results from* just background conditions. Rather, the just distribution of free time instead must be recognized as *a component of* just background conditions.

Specifically, I argue that justice requires that all citizens have a fair share of free time. Citizens have legitimate claims to free time on the basis of the *effective freedoms principle*, a foundational tenet of liberal egalitarian justice, which holds that citizens have legitimate claims to a fair share of the resources that are generally required to exercise their formal liberties and opportunities. In the same way that citizens generally require the resources of income and wealth to exercise their freedoms, so too do they generally require the resource of free time. To have their fair shares of free time, citizens must have time not committed to the necessities of life, time they can predictably use for their own ends, and time they can share with other citizens. Ensuring a just distribution of income and wealth is insufficient to guarantee such a just distribution of free time, and so our theories of justice and our public policies must treat free time as a distinct object of distributive concern to guarantee citizens "hours for what we will."

1.3 OVERVIEW

The argument begins, in Chapter 2, with the analytical framework, that of liberal proceduralism, and its distinction between specific goods and resources. Surveying the neglect of leisure or free time in contemporary theories of justice, I argue that this neglect owes to the way that political philosophers in general, and liberal egalitarians in particular, have conceptualized leisure as a specific good. Generally, leisure has been understood as either time engaged in philosophical contemplation or recreational activities, or time not engaged in paid work. As a specific good, leisure is presumptively not an appropriate object of concern for a liberal theory of justice. This understanding of leisure time is, however, unjustifiably limited, for it neglects the way in which time is also a resource. (To distinguish these ideas, I refer to leisure when understood as a specific good and free time when understood as a resource.)

Chapter 3 constructs this conception of free time as a resource. To be a resource, and thus an appropriate concern of a liberal theory of justice, free time must, first, be a necessary input for the pursuit of a wide range of individual ends and, second, be measurable in a way that meets the constraints of a public and feasible theory of justice. I argue for a particular conception that meets these criteria and is properly a resource: free time, understood as time not committed to meeting one's own, or one's dependents', basic needs, whether with necessary paid work, household labor, or personal care. Citizens generally require free time, so understood, to pursue their conceptions of the good, whatever they may be.

In Chapter 4, the book's normative core, I argue that all citizens are entitled to a fair share of free time on the basis of the effective freedoms principle. Without the means to make use of them, citizens' freedoms are of little value. As I show, citizens generally require free time to exercise their formal freedoms, whether to participate in politics, practice their religions, or do almost anything they are legally free to do. Thus, on the basis of the effective freedoms principle, citizens have legitimate claims to free time.

Furthermore, I argue that, in order to ensure that citizens have their fair shares of free time, our theories of justice and public policies must treat time as a distinct object of distributive concern. Contrary to a widely held assumption, the time-money substitutability claim, realizing a just distribution of income and wealth is *not* sufficient to ensure a just distribution of free time. Neither of the assumptions on which this claim depends, the perfect divisibility of labor demand and the perfect substitutability of money and basic needs satisfaction, obtains, as a consequence of both empirical and ethical limitations of economic markets. As such, how much free time citizens have must be separately assessed, and a just distribution of free time must be realized through specifically targeted interventions.

Chapters 5 and 6 extend the arguments of the preceding chapters to two areas, freedom of association and gender and caregiving. Chapter 5 shows

that, on the basis of the effective freedoms principle, citizens are also entitled to periods of shared free time because such time is generally required to
have effective freedom of association. The central exercises of freedom of association, whether civic, religious, or intimate, depend on sharing time together. As such, potential associates face a temporal coordination problem.
I consider three possible solutions—a universal basic income, mandated work
hours flexibility, and a common period of free time—and I argue that the
third may be the most effective and feasible for circumstances proximate to
our own. Drawing on the arguments of the justices of the U.S. Supreme
Court in *McGowan v. Maryland* (1961), I argue that Sunday closing laws,
in a modified form consistent with economic and religious freedom, are a
means of realizing effective freedom of association.

Chapter 6 turns to gender and caregiving, and shows how recognizing citizens' claims to free time contributes to a liberal egalitarian theory of gender
justice. I argue that gender justice requires that men and women not only have
free choices from among equal options, but also choose from among just
background conditions. One of those conditions is that all citizens must have
their fair shares of free time, with caregiving for children and other dependents treated as a necessary activity like necessary paid work. I show how
this entails that citizens must be able to choose to engage in paid work and
caregiving and still have free time, as realized through a set of workplace
accommodations for parents and other caregivers. Gender justice requires,
apart from the conditions for free choice and equal options, that men and
women choose their household responsibilities from among these just background conditions.

The final chapter addresses how to provide free time. For citizens to possess their fair shares of free time, they must both have their fair amount of
free time, and have it under fair conditions to make effective use of it, with
access to generally usable periods of free time on a predictable schedule. Addressing the question of how to provide free time demonstrates how recognizing citizens' claims to free time provides grounds, first, to support both
a range of contested welfare and employment policies and distinctive labor
regulations and, second, to challenge the presumption in favor of unceasing
economic growth as a social goal.

Several features of the argument warrant emphasis at the outset. First,
the core argument—that citizens are entitled to a fair share of free time—
applies to any theory that is committed to ensuring that citizens possess the
means to exercise their freedoms. All liberal egalitarian theories share this

commitment, and the argument is developed within this approach. Liberal egalitarianism, however, encompasses a broad family of views, which combine the dual values of liberty and equality in a variety of ways. So that the core argument applies broadly to any theory that holds this commitment, it is constructed to not depend on taking a particular position on a range of contested issues within this family of views. (These points of divergence notably include the scope and site of justice, the significance of individual responsibility, and the appropriate distributive principle and metric.) After establishing the core argument, in extending the argument in later chapters, I do take positions on some of these issues, but one who takes different positions could develop the argument in ways other than I do here. Indeed, once recognized as an all-purpose resource, free time ought to be incorporated in various ways across different theories of justice.

Second, to the extent that liberals have attended to the distribution of leisure, they have generally done so on the grounds of some special justification. Work-hours regulations, for instance, are variously defended on the grounds that they are necessary to protect workers from coercion and exploitation, to prevent unhealthy and unsafe working conditions, to reduce unemployment, and to address gender inequality, among others.[7] While these may be sound arguments, they are of limited force and scope. My aim is to show that citizens' claims to free time do not depend on such exceptional or contingent justifications. Instead, without relying on these special justifications, citizens are entitled to free time on the grounds of a foundational principle of liberal egalitarian justice.

Third, the argument assumes and is consistent with the commitments to anti-paternalism, non-perfectionism, and neutrality underlying the liberal proceduralist approach. It holds that citizens are entitled to free time to devote to their own pursuits, whatever those may be. Within the bounds of the law, one's free time is one's to use as one sees fit. Citizens' claims to free time are not conditional on how they spend it.

For some, this may raise the worry that citizens will squander their free time on unproductive or unfulfilling activities—consistent with headlines

---

7 See, for instance, Jon C. Messenger, "Towards Decent Working Time," in *Decent Working Time: New Trends, New Issues*, ed. Jean-Yves Boulin, Michel Lallement, Jon C. Messenger, and François Michon (Geneva: International Labour Office, 2006), 419–41 and Allard E. Dembe, "Ethical Issues Relating to the Health Effects of Long Working Hours," *Journal of Business Ethics* 84 (2009): 195–208.

like "Americans Are Spending More Time Watching TV and Sleeping"—
and the objection that citizens should be constrained or induced to make
meaningful use of their free time.[8] In response to this objection, first to the
empirical claim, it cannot be assumed that people would use their free time
as they presently do if all had their fair share under just conditions. The
fact that someone spends her little free time watching television when she
is exhausted by long hours of work or when her friends and family are all
working does not give us reliable information about how she would use her
free time under other conditions. Moreover, it is possible for the argument
to be paired, consistent with liberal neutrality, with state support for free
time infrastructure—parks, recreation facilities, the arts—as underprovided
public goods. More generally, I argue for citizens' entitlement to free time
within demanding anti-paternalist and non-perfectionist constraints in part
to establish that even if one holds to these demanding liberal constraints,
citizens still have claims to free time. In extending the argument, one could
modify it with paternalist or perfectionist conditions to constrain or encourage people to use their free time in certain ways. Nonetheless, my position
remains that citizens are entitled to free time to devote to their own ends,
whatever those may be.

Finally, following the standard application of the effective freedoms principle, I argue that citizens have claims to free time as members of separate
political societies (and I focus on the United States). There is no reason the
argument could not be extended to establish an international or universal
claim to free time, however, if consistent with one's position on human
rights or the boundaries of distributive justice.

1.4 FREE TIME IN THE CONTEMPORARY UNITED STATES

Before proceeding to the argument, it may be useful to briefly describe
some relevant features of the distribution of free time in the contemporary
United States. In contrast to widely cited figures on unemployment, material
poverty, and income and wealth inequality, popular awareness of the extent

---

8 Justin Lahart and Emmeline Zhao, "What Would You Do With an Extra Hour? Americans Are Spending More Time Watching TV and Sleeping as Unemployment Rises, Survey
Finds," *Wall Street Journal*, eastern ed., June 23, 2010.

to which many people must devote long hours to necessary tasks and have little free time is often limited to personal experience. Though existing empirical data on work hours and time use do not perfectly track the relevant sense of free time, understood as time not committed to necessary paid work, household labor, or personal care, they nonetheless still provide an illuminating indication of how many people have little free time.[9]

First, many Americans spend long hours in paid work. According to recent data, almost one-third of employed Americans work more than forty-five hours per week and about one-eighth more than fifty-five hours per week. While some portion of these workers want to work such hours, they are in the minority. Over 80 percent of those working more than fifty hours per week would prefer to work shorter hours, with those working fifty to sixty hours per week preferring on average to work thirteen hours less and those working more than sixty hours preferring to work twenty-five hours less.[10]

The preference to spend less time working is not limited to those with long hours. Among all employed Americans, 60 percent would prefer shorter work hours. These workers, however, face financial and institutional barriers to acting on their stated preferences, as I discuss in Chapter 4. Of those who would prefer to work less, over half report that they do not because they cannot afford to, and another substantial portion report that they do not because their employer would not allow them to reduce their hours. Apart from the problems of unemployment and underemployment, many workers are overemployed: they would prefer to work shorter hours even for a corresponding reduction in pay.[11]

---

9 The existing time-use data do not perfectly correspond to the distinction between free time and necessary time, as I discuss in Chapter 3, because they generally measure how much time one spends overall in a particular activity, without specifying what portion of time engaged in an activity is necessary to meet one's own, or one's dependents', basic needs.

10 Daniel S. Hamermesh and Elena Stancanelli, "Long Workweeks and Strange Hours," *ILR Review* 68 (2015): 1009; Jerry A. Jacobs and Kathleen Gerson, *The Time Divide: Work, Family, and Gender Inequality* (Cambridge, MA: Harvard University Press, 2004), 64–67. As with all such survey data measuring stated preferences, these data, and the other survey results cited in this section, have limitations, but are still highly informative, especially given the institutional and methodological barriers to measuring revealed preferences on these subjects (for instance, on the inability of workers to actually select their preferred work hours, see 4.4).

11 Jacobs and Gerson, *Time Divide*, 64, 74–75; Lonnie Golden and Tesfayi Gebreselassie, "Overemployment Mismatches: The Preference for Fewer Hours of Work," *Monthly Labor Review* 130 (2007): 18–37.

Of course being employed itself carries many important benefits, and the problems of unemployment and underemployment are rightly central concerns. But among those who are employed, long work hours and over-employment have been linked to a range of possible negative impacts on well-being. Specifically, long hours of work are associated with a broad set of adverse physical and mental health outcomes, including cardiovascular and musculoskeletal disorders, diabetes, obesity, alcohol abuse, depression, fatigue, and reduced cognitive and executive function.[12] Furthermore, being overemployed has a negative association with health and life satisfaction, with overemployed workers reporting worse health than those working the same number of hours.[13]

Long work hours occur across the occupational spectrum. The more educated and those who work in professional, technical, and managerial occupations are disproportionately represented among long-hours workers.[14] Yet, significant portions of the less educated also work long hours. One-eighth of employed men with less than a high school degree work more than fifty hours and one-fifth of employed men with only a high school degree work more than fifty hours per week. Moreover, while in relative terms white-collar workers are more likely to work long hours, in absolute terms white-collar workers still constitute less than half of those working long hours. Over half of those working more than fifty hours per week are not professionals or managers and over half of those working more than fifty hours per week have less than a college degree.[15] Furthermore, only 50 percent of those in the lowest wage quartile receive any paid vacation days or holidays, while 90 per-

---

12 Sibyl Kleiner and Eliza K. Pavalko, "Clocking In: The Organization of Work Time and Health in the United States," *Social Forces* 88 (2010): 1463–86; Claire C. Caruso, "Possible Broad Impacts of Long Work Hours," *Industrial Health* 44 (2006): 531–36; Kate Sparks, Cary Cooper, Yitzhak Fried, and Arie Shirom, "The Effects of Hours of Work on Health: A Meta-analytic Review," *Journal of Occupational and Organizational Psychology* 70 (1997): 391–408. As with all such associational claims based on observational data, the degree to which causation can reasonably be inferred varies across studies.

13 Cem Başlevent and Hasan Kirmanoğlu, "The Impact of Deviations from Desired Hours of Work on the Life Satisfaction of Employees," *Social Indicators Research* 118 (2014): 33–43; David Bell, Steffen Otterbach, and Alfonso Sousa-Poza, "Work Hours Constraints and Health," *Annals of Economics and Statistics* 105/106 (2012): 35–54.

14 It is worth revisiting Thorstein Veblen's famous depiction of the leisure class, in light of present circumstances. Thorstein Veblen, *The Theory of the Leisure Class* (1899; repr., New York: Penguin, 1979); see Jonathan Gershuny, "Veblen in Reverse: Evidence from the Multinational Time-Use Archive," *Social Indicators Research* 93 (2009): 37–45.

15 Jacobs and Gerson, *Time Divide*, 34–36.

cent of those in the highest wage quartile do, with an average gap of ten vacation days between low-wage and high-wage workers.[16]

Apart from long work hours, many work outside the "standard" weekday daytime work schedule. Over one-third of employed Americans work on weekends, with 8 percent regularly working seven days a week. On a typical day, over one-quarter of American employees perform some work between ten in the evening and six in the morning. Of employees, 8 percent regularly work evenings, 4 percent regularly work night shifts, and 8 percent have variable or rotating work hours. Around one-quarter of employees face mandatory overtime work.[17] Moreover, though those with more education and higher earnings disproportionately work long hours, they are more likely to work during standard hours. It is those with less education and lower earnings who disproportionately perform evening and night work, with lower-wage workers more likely to work evenings and nights even among managerial and clerical workers alone.[18]

Of course, people also spend many hours on unpaid household and caregiving labor, maintaining their homes and caring for children, parents, relatives, and other members of their communities. The American Time Use Survey, which measures the amount of time people spend engaged in various activities, shows that Americans spend on average around twenty hours per week on household production (cooking, cleaning, grocery shopping, vehicle and home maintenance, etc.).[19] In addition, over one-fifth of American households have children under age twelve and one-eighth have children under age six, and those who live with children under age six spend on average two hours per day providing primary child care and an additional five hours per day providing supervisory child care.[20] Furthermore, one-sixth of

16 Bureau of Labor Statistics, "Employee Benefits in the United States—March 2015" (news release, July 24, 2015), 15; Rebecca Ray, Milla Sanes, and John Schmitt, "No-Vacation Nation Revisited" (Center for Economic and Policy Research, 2013), 1.

17 Hamermesh and Stancanelli, "Long Workweeks and Strange Hours," 1009–10; Harriet B. Presser, *Working in a 24/7 Economy: Challenges for American Families* (New York: Russell Sage, 2003), 15–17; Lonnie Golden and Barbara Wiens-Tuers, "Mandatory Overtime Work in the United States: Who, Where, What?," *Labor Studies Journal* 30 (2005): 9.

18 Daniel S. Hamermesh, "Changing Inequality in Work Injuries and Work Timing," *Monthly Labor Review* 122 (1999): 23–27.

19 J. Steven Landefeld, Barbara M. Fraumeni, and Cindy M. Vojtech, "Accounting for Household Production: A Prototype Satellite Account Using the American Time Use Survey," *Review of Income and Wealth* 55 (2009): 209.

20 Jonathan Vespa, Jamie M. Lewis, and Rose M. Kreider, "America's Families and Living Arrangements: 2012" (Current Population Reports, P20-570; Washington, DC: U.S. Census

adults, or forty million people, provide unpaid elder care, and almost half of these caregivers are also employed full-time.[21]

While the total workloads of men and women—combining paid work, unpaid household labor, and family care, and averaging across employment, marital, and parental categories—are similar, they still significantly vary by gender.[22] Mothers, on average, do about half as much paid work as fathers do, while fathers do about half as much unpaid household labor and family care as mothers do.[23] Moreover, the overall parity in the total workloads obscures significant inequalities across comparable groups of men and women. Full-time employed married mothers of young children, for instance, do more total work than comparable fathers. Though these mothers do somewhat less paid work than full-time employed married fathers of young children, they do an offsettingly greater amount of unpaid household labor and child care, to the effect that they do an additional five hours of work per week. While this does not constitute a full "second shift," it remains a considerable disparity.[24]

When time-use studies incorporate respondents' affective experiences of various activities, they find that paid work, housework, and caring for children and adults are among the activities people find least enjoyable and interesting. By contrast, the activities people most enjoy include socializing, relaxing, playing sports and exercising, and praying.[25] Not surprisingly, when asked if they could change the way they spend their time, over two-

Bureau, 2013), 4; Bureau of Labor Statistics, "American Time Use Survey—2014 Results" (news release, June 24, 2015).

21 Bureau of Labor Statistics, "Unpaid Eldercare in the United States" (news release, September 23, 2015).

22 Kimberly Fisher, Muriel Egerton, Jonathan I. Gershuny, and John P. Robinson, "Gender Convergence in the American Heritage Time Use Study (AHTUS)," *Social Indicators Research* 82 (2007): 1–33. See also Marybeth J. Mattingly and Suzanne M. Bianchi, "Gender Differences in the Quantity and Quality of Free Time: The U.S. Experience," *Social Forces* 81 (2003): 999–1030 and Mark Aguiar and Erik Hurst, "Measuring Trends in Leisure: The Allocation of Time over Five Decades," *Quarterly Journal of Economics* 122 (2007): 969–1006.

23 Suzanne M. Bianchi, "Family Change and Time Allocation in American Families," *Annals of the American Academy of Political and Social Science* 638 (2011): 27, 29.

24 Melissa A. Milkie, Sara B. Raley, and Suzanne M. Bianchi, "Taking on the Second Shift: Time Allocations and Time Pressures of U.S. Parents with Preschoolers," *Social Forces* 88 (2009): 499. Cf. Arlie Russell Hochschild, *The Second Shift* (New York: Avon Books, 1989).

25 Alan B. Krueger, Daniel Kahneman, David Schkade, Norbert Schwarz, and Arthur A. Stone, "National Time Accounting: The Currency of Life," in *Measuring the Subjective Well-Being of Nations: National Accounts of Time Use and Well-Being*, ed. Alan B. Krueger (Chicago: University of Chicago Press, 2009), 42–47; Daniel Kahneman and Alan B. Krueger, "Devel-

thirds of Americans report that they would prefer to spend more time in leisure activities, with about two-thirds preferring more time with friends, and about four-fifths preferring more time with family.[26]

Moreover, these disparities in how much free time people have matter for political participation: those who have more free time are more likely to vote and to engage in more time-consuming political acts (contacting government officials, working on a campaign, serving on local governing boards, and attending board meetings), and among those most active in politics, more free time is associated with more political participation.[27]

Though I focus on the United States, these phenomena are not uniquely American. American employees are more likely to work long hours than workers in parts of Western Europe (including France, Germany, and the Netherlands), but the rates of long work hours are similar in other Organisation for Economic Co-operation and Development countries (including the United Kingdom, Switzerland, Israel, Australia, New Zealand, Japan, Korea, and Mexico). Globally, it is estimated that 22 percent of workers around the world work more than forty-eight hours per week.[28] Moreover, comparing the United States only to Western Europe, the rates of weekend and night work are, though lower, still high, the disparities in total workloads between comparable men and women the same, and the proportions of those who report a preference for more time in leisure activities and with family and friends similar.[29]

---

opments in the Measurement of Subjective Well-Being," *Journal of Economic Perspectives* 20 (2006): 13.

26 Tom W. Smith, "A Cross-National Comparison on Attitudes towards Work by Age and Labor Force Status" (Organisation for Economic Co-operation and Development, December 2000), 17–18.

27 Henry E. Brady, Sidney Verba, and Kay Lehman Schlozman, "Beyond SES: A Resource Model of Political Participation," *American Political Science Review* 89 (1995): 283–84.

28 Hamermesh and Stancanelli, "Long Workweeks and Strange Hours," 1009; Sangheon Lee, Deirdre McCann, and Jon C. Messenger, *Working Time around the World: Trends in Working Hours, Laws, and Policies in a Global Comparative Perspective* (New York: Routledge, 2007), 46–51, 53. For an account of how work hours in the United States and Western Europe were similar up until 1970, and why they have diverged since, see Alberto Alesina, Edward Glaeser, and Bruce Sacerdote, "Work and Leisure in the United States and Europe: Why So Different?," in *NBER Macroeconomics Annual 2005*, ed. Mark Gertler and Kenneth Rogoff (Cambridge, MA: MIT Press, 2006), 1–64. I address how the argument applies to societies at varying levels of development in 7.2.

29 Hamermesh and Stancanelli, "Long Workweeks and Strange Hours," 1009; Jose Ignacio Gimenez-Nadal and Almudena Sevilla-Sanz, "The Time-Crunch Paradox," *Social Indicators Research* 102 (2011): 189; Smith, "Cross-National Comparison on Attitudes towards Work," 17–18.

Before I turn from the empirical to the normative, one final point to make is that, though this book is a work of political theory, the extent to which many people today have little free time is its motivation, and the arguments to follow aim to provide normative guidance and principled grounds to address this lack of free time in policy and practice.

CHAPTER 2

LEISURE AS A SPECIFIC GOOD

2.1 THE NEGLECT OF TIME

On the basis of a survey of recent research—finding that many Americans report they have too little time for leisure activities and wish they spent less time working, that spending a greater amount of time in leisure pursuits and activities of one's own choosing is associated with better, and long work hours with worse, health and subjective well-being, that there are significant inequalities in the distribution of free time, and that these inequalities are associated with inequalities in political participation—one might expect that leisure or free time would be a central concern in liberal theories of distributive justice.[1] Such theories are typically concerned with things that citizens generally want or need, that are associated with gains to individual well-being, that are distributed unequally, and that are associated with political participation. To be clear, these empirical findings are not, in themselves, sufficient to conclude that leisure or free time ought to be an object of distributive concern. They nonetheless provide at least reason to assess whether and how the unequal distribution of leisure or free time ought be addressed. Yet liberal egalitarians have in fact given the subject little attention, and what little attention they have paid leisure or free time treats it as far from a central concern.

1 See 1.4 for a survey of this research. I refer to liberal theories of distributive justice and liberal egalitarianism interchangeably. I use "liberal" and "egalitarian" broadly: "liberals" need only give special priority to a set of individual freedoms and "egalitarians" need only value some type of social or distributive equality.

In this chapter, I contend that it is the way that leisure has standardly been conceptualized that has led to its neglect by theorists of distributive justice. That is, leisure has been regarded as a *specific good*. In particular, leisure has been understood as (1) time engaged in intrinsically valuable activities, namely philosophical contemplation, (2) time engaged in play or recreation, or (3) time not engaged in paid work. The standard liberal egalitarian approach to the distribution of such specific goods—*liberal proceduralism*—is to ensure that all citizens have *fair access* to such goods by ensuring a fair distribution of all-purpose resources.[2] In possession of their share of such resources, individuals can choose which specific goods to select in accordance with their own preferences and understandings of the good life. For the liberal state to do otherwise and to ensure a given distribution of specific goods themselves, or even to promote access to one specific good over others, without some special intervening justification, is to overstep its bounds and to violate the rightful deference given to individual autonomy.

Thus, on the standard liberal proceduralist approach, as long as all citizens have access to the specific good of leisure time, understood according to one of the three standard conceptions, it would be prima facie wrong for the state to aim to ensure any particular distribution of leisure. Instead, the just distribution of leisure time is whatever emerges as a result of individuals' choices made in accordance with their conceptions of the good, depending, that is, on the value they give to contemplation, or play, or paid work relative to other specific goods, assuming all have access to such goods. The appropriate focus of distributive concern is, accordingly, not on the distribution of the specific good of leisure, but on the distribution of the all-purpose resources that ensure that citizens have access to such goods, resources such as education, income and wealth, and occupational opportunities. So, assuming (1) the legitimacy of the liberal proceduralist approach, (2) the absence of an intervening justification for treating the specific good of leisure differently, and (3) the validity of the standard conception of leisure as a specific good, it is indeed appropriate for distributive theorists to disregard the types of findings presented at the outset and to continue to disregard leisure time.

I do not, however, believe that theorists of distributive justice have been right to dismiss all of the empirical findings above and, more important, to

---

2 This statement of liberal proceduralism does privilege a "resourcist" theory of distributive justice, but it is, as I discuss below, not inconsistent with theories that use other distributive metrics.

neglect the distribution of free time. In order to substantiate such a contention, one could reject (1), (2), or (3). I will not reject (1), as I instead endorse and assume the legitimacy of the liberal proceduralist approach to distributive justice. I also will not reject (2), though some of the claims I advance in the course of the argument would provide effective grounds to take this approach as a supplementary path. Instead, I take route (3): I reject the standard conception of leisure time as a specific good. My argument is not that leisure cannot be appropriately understood as a specific good according to one of the standard conceptions; rather, I argue that the understandings of leisure as a specific good do not exhaust the possible conceptions of leisure. That is, I argue, leisure time should be understood not only as a specific good, but also as itself a *resource*—as the *resource of free time*. Accordingly, from this point on, I will distinguish between leisure and free time, referring to leisure for the concept as a specific good and to free time for the concept as a resource. I argue that free time, when understood as a resource, is central to liberal theories of justice.

That, ultimately, is the core of my argument. The aims of this chapter, however, are more preliminary. I begin with a discussion of how leisure has been neglected by liberal theories of justice, and then examine the liberal proceduralist approach and the distinction between specific goods and resources. I present the standard conceptions of leisure as a specific good, before suggesting how to conceptualize free time as a resource. The argument for understanding free time as a resource is the subject of Chapter 3.

In liberal theories of justice, free time or leisure—or even time generally—is rarely mentioned or given more than passing notice.[3] There are, to my knowledge, only three places where one finds any sustained consideration of leisure as an object of distributive concern: Michael Walzer's treatment of "free time" as a distinct "sphere of justice," John Rawls's consideration of including leisure in the index of "social primary goods," and discussion

---

3 How justice applies to work is also relatively neglected, though work has received more attention than leisure or free time. In treatments of just work, leisure is sometimes suggested as possible compensation for a lack of meaningful work, e.g., Russell Muirhead, *Just Work* (Cambridge, MA: Harvard University Press, 2004), 174. See also Richard J. Arneson, "Meaningful Work and Market Socialism," *Ethics* 97 (1987): 517–45; Samuel Arnold, "The Difference Principle at Work," *Journal of Political Philosophy* 20 (2012): 94–118; Nien-Hê Hsieh, "Justice in Production," *Journal of Political Philosophy* 16 (2008): 72–100; James Bernard Murphy, *The Moral Economy of Labor: Aristotelian Themes in Economic Theory* (New Haven: Yale University Press, 1993); Adina Schwartz, "Meaningful Work," *Ethics* 92 (1982): 634–46; Lucas Stanczyk, "Productive Justice," *Philosophy & Public Affairs* 40 (2012): 144–64.

of the "right to rest and leisure" in the Universal Declaration of Human Rights.[4] When the subject does receive such attention, the arguments are in fact about another subject (namely, the obligation to work) with leisure serving merely as a convenient proxy, are narrowly limited in the positions they advance, or are generally dismissive. The few existing treatments of the distribution of leisure may give one little reason to think it is a subject that merits much further consideration.

Free Time as a Sphere of Justice

Walzer's theory of distributive justice is one of "complex equality," according to which all distinct social goods—such as money, office, recognition, and political office—ought to be distributed based on principles specific to each good within separate "spheres of justice." Walzer recognizes free time as one of the distinct social goods that merits its own sphere of justice, and indeed Walzer contends that the "distribution of free time" is a "central issue of distributive justice."

The particular principles that Walzer advances to govern the distribution of free time do not, however, substantiate this claim. Walzer makes two arguments in particular that moderate the claim's impact. First, though he contends that individuals do need a "cessation from work," he argues that the particular way that free time is distributed in a society is not a matter of justice. Instead, it is a matter of societal discretion: one society could grant individuals the leave to take personal vacations while another society could coercively impose public holidays. The choice between these two types of distribution is not governed by principles of justice. Though the provision of free time in some form remains a matter of concern, setting aside the question of what form that provision takes effectively reduces the reach of justice over free time.

Second, and more important, Walzer suggests that if complex equality obtained, to the effect that money, offices, education, and political power were more equally distributed than they are at present, significant inequalities in free time would not arise. The rich would not be able to amass enough wealth to enjoy their familiar "upper-class idleness" and the powerful would not hold enough sway to command others to work while they rest. Instead, Walzer as-

---

4 Philippe Van Parijs's argument for a universal basic income—with the implication that one could spend all of one's days in idleness, surfing and the like—may seem like a relevant consideration of leisure and it is indeed indirectly related to leisure, but it is not, as I discuss below, actually concerned with the distribution of leisure itself.

sumes that realizing complex equality in the other spheres of justice would automatically go a long way toward achieving a more equal distribution of free time. By virtue of this assumption, Walzer again blunts the impact of recognizing the distribution of free time as a central concern of justice.

Having tempered his position in these ways, Walzer ultimately contends that justice requires only that one not "be excluded from the forms of rest central to one's own time and place." Given that this principle must be flexible enough to apply to diverse societies' different ways of organizing free time, it is unclear what this principle demands in practice. Moreover, given that justice—on either Walzer's view or any liberal egalitarian view—would already require some form of equal social status, and that, as Walzer contends, the greater equality required in money and political power would mitigate existing inequalities in free time, it is unclear what, if anything, this principle demands beyond the other requirements of justice. Free time, on this account, might be an important domain of human life, but it is likely not one that a theory of justice must treat as a "central issue."[5]

Leisure as a Primary Good

The only other notable treatment of leisure within theories of distributive justice—Rawls's consideration of leisure as a primary good—is not in fact directly about leisure. That is, Rawls suggests that leisure could be added to the index of social primary goods (the metric used to compare individuals' social and economic advantages) neither because leisure is an important good nor because the distribution of leisure is a relevant component of the distribution of social advantage. Instead, Rawls proposes recognizing leisure as a primary good only as one possible way of remedying a flaw he perceived in

5 Michael Walzer, *Spheres of Justice: A Defense of Pluralism and Equality* (New York: Basic Books, 1983), 187, 185, 196. Perhaps for these reasons, Walzer's claim that the distribution of free time is a central issue of distributive justice has not been endorsed or developed. As one indication of the silence that has met Walzer's treatment of free time, a prominent edited volume dedicated to *Spheres of Justice*, with essays by many of the central figures in the distributive justice literature, contains only two references to free time, even though one of those references describes Walzer's discussion of free time as "one of the best chapters in the book." Brian Barry, "Spherical Justice and Global Injustice," in *Pluralism, Justice, and Equality*, ed. David Miller and Michael Walzer (Oxford: Oxford University Press, 1995), 73. The other reference is in Amy Gutmann's essay "Justice Across the Spheres," 112. Both Barry and Gutmann discuss free time to make more general points; neither endorses Walzer's contention that free time is a central issue of distributive justice.

his original theory, that is, that the theory did not sufficiently incorporate the expectation that all citizens should work.

In the first statement of his theory of justice, "justice as fairness," Rawls addresses neither leisure nor a work expectation.[6] He proposes that inequalities in social and economic advantages ought to be distributed so that they are to the greatest benefit of the least advantaged (the difference principle), and that the relevant metric for determining advantages is an index of primary goods. The index consists in a subset of all social primary goods, and includes income and wealth and the powers and prerogatives of office. When the difference principle and the index are so formulated, absent some further clarification, an implication is that those who do not work and do not earn an income, even if they willingly do not do so, qualify as among the least advantaged and thus require public support. This implication was first pressed on Rawls by the economist R. A. Musgrave, who argued that the theory as formulated "favors those with a high preference for leisure," including "recluses, saints, and (nonconsulting) scholars." Rawls accepted the force of Musgrave's critique and in his initial reply and subsequent elaborations considered how to ensure that those who elected not to work did not qualify as among the least advantaged.[7]

It is in this context that Rawls considered adding leisure to the index of primary goods. Specifically, he proposed that "twenty-four hours less a standard working day might be included in the index as leisure," so that "those who are unwilling to work would have a standard working day of extra leisure, and this extra leisure itself would be stipulated as equivalent to the index of primary goods of the least advantaged," to the effect that those who choose not to work do not count as the least advantaged. Rawls consistently maintained that those "who surf all day off Malibu" must somehow support themselves and cannot live off public funds, and that adding leisure to the index is one way of ensuring this result.[8]

6 John Rawls, *A Theory of Justice*, original ed. (Cambridge, MA: Belknap, 1971).

7 R. A. Musgrave, "Maximin, Uncertainty, and the Leisure Trade-Off," *Quarterly Journal of Economics* 88 (1974): 632; John Rawls, "Reply to Alexander and Musgrave," *Quarterly Journal of Economics* 88 (1974): 654. Rawls returned to the question in "The Priority of Right and Ideas of the Good," *Philosophy & Public Affairs* 17 (1988): 257 and in *Justice as Fairness: A Restatement*, ed. Erin Kelly (Cambridge, MA: Belknap, 2001), 179. The revised version of "The Priority of Right and Ideas of the Good" in *Political Liberalism* (New York: Columbia University Press, 1993), 173–211 includes modest revisions of the discussion of leisure from the earlier version of the article (at 181–82).

8 Rawls, "Priority of Right and Ideas of the Good" (1988), 257n7. Rawls consistently uses the example of the Malibu surfer in his discussions of leisure (see also *Justice as Fairness*, 179,

It is worth stressing that Rawls never contended that leisure *ought* to be included in the index, only that doing so was *one possible strategy* among others to ensure that all "do their part in sharing the burdens of social life." Rawls did not discuss leisure's importance or its distribution, and indeed his willingness to include leisure in the index was apparently not prompted by a concern for either (aside from his opposition to supporting the leisure of surfers with welfare). Instead, Rawls argued that leisure ought to be added to the index of primary goods *only if* it would be "the best way to express the idea that all citizens are to do their part in society's cooperative work." By implication, if including leisure in the index would not be the best way to incorporate a work expectation, then leisure ought not be given that status and another strategy ought to be pursued. (One such alternative strategy that Rawls suggests is simply "to assume that everyone works a standard working day.") Far from constituting an endorsement of Walzer's claim that the distribution of free time is a central concern of distributive justice, Rawls's willingness to recognize leisure as a primary good is in fact only instrumental to grounding a work expectation.[9]

A Human Right to Leisure

Article 24 of the Universal Declaration of Human Rights holds that "everyone has the right to rest and leisure, including reasonable limitation of working hours and periodic holidays with pay." On its face, this recognition of a human right to leisure seems to undermine the contention that leisure has been neglected by contemporary theories of justice, for if anything does, the canonization of a fundamental interest as a human right seems to indicate the widespread acceptance of that right as a fundamental principle of justice. In fact, however, Article 24 is widely criticized and even mocked; it is,

---

and "Priority of Right and Ideas of the Good" [1993], 181–82). Philippe Van Parijs recounts that when he and Rawls had a conversation about the issue in 1987, the Malibu surfer was the example to which they referred (Van Parijs, "Why Surfers Should Be Fed: The Liberal Case for an Unconditional Basic Income," *Philosophy & Public Affairs* 20 [1991]: 101).

9 Rawls, *Justice as Fairness*, 179. For helpful discussions of Rawls's treatment of leisure, see Philippe Van Parijs, "Difference Principles," in *The Cambridge Companion to Rawls*, ed. Samuel Freeman (Cambridge: Cambridge University Press, 2003) and *Real Freedom for All: What (if Anything) Can Justify Capitalism?* (Oxford: Oxford University Press, 1995), 92–102; Thomas W. Pogge, *Realizing Rawls* (Ithaca: Cornell University Press, 1989), 198–200; Samuel Freeman, *Rawls* (London: Routledge, 2007), 229–30; and Kristi A. Olson, "Leisure," in *The Cambridge Rawls Lexicon*, ed. Jon Mandle and David A. Reidy (Cambridge: Cambridge University Press, 2015), 433–34.

indeed, "mirth-producing." One recent commentator summarizes the usual treatment of the human right to leisure by noting that though "it is an official affirmation by a highly respected international organization, almost everyone has regarded it as suspect."[10]

Some who reject the human right to leisure also reject all of the "second generational" human rights to economic and social conditions that are recognized by the declaration. Maurice Cranston, for instance, argues that only fundamental political and civil rights ought to be recognized as human rights because going further and recognizing economic and social rights effectively devalues the currency of human rights, and in pressing this critique Cranston singles out the right to holidays with pay as particularly objectionable. Even those who accept economic and social rights as justifiable human rights, however, and who endorse many of the other second generational rights in the declaration, often find Article 24 a stroke too far. Allen Buchanan, for instance, advocates a human right to "resources for subsistence" but rejects the right to leisure as one of the "more dubious putative economic rights." Buchanan captures the widespread dismissal of Article 24 when he refers to the right to holidays with pay as "notorious" and "pretty obvious[ly] . . . not necessary for a decent human life."[11]

Though the right to leisure is widely rejected as a proper or genuine human right, it must be noted that Article 24 is not without its defenders. Jeremy Waldron, for one, criticizes those who dismiss the right to leisure, arguing that "in the history of labor's struggle with capital," the attempt to secure limitations on working hours "has been a constant and desperate theme, and anyone who denigrates its urgency simply doesn't know what he is talking about." Although Waldron offers a forceful argument against any dismissal

10 Sidney Hook, "Reflections on Human Rights," in *Philosophy and Public Policy* (Carbondale: Southern Illinois University Press, 1980), 92, cited in Mathias Risse, "A Right to Work? A Right to Leisure? Labor Rights as Human Rights," *Law & Ethics of Human Rights* 3 (2009): 1n4; Carl Wellman, *The Proliferation of Rights: Moral Progress or Empty Rhetoric* (Boulder, CO: Westview, 1999), 2.

11 Maurice Cranston imagines that recognizing a right to leisure might lead people to say, for instance, "It would be a splendid thing . . . for everyone to have holidays with pay, a splendid thing for everyone to have social security, a splendid thing to have fair trials, free speech, and the right to life—and one day, perhaps, all these beautiful ideals will be realized." Cranston, "Are There Any Human Rights?," *Daedalus* 112 (1983): 12. See also Cranston, "Human Rights, Real and Supposed," in *Political Theory and the Rights of Man*, ed. D. D. Raphael (London: Macmillan, 1967), 43–53 and *What Are Human Rights?* (London: Bodley Head, 1973). Allen Buchanan, *Justice, Legitimacy, and Self-Determination: Moral Foundations for International Law* (Oxford: Oxford University Press, 2004), 160, 129.

of the right to leisure out of hand as unjustified, his remarks are limited to that aim and he does not provide a further positive account of why leisure ought to be recognized as a human right or what the recognition of such a right would entail. Despite the modesty of Waldron's position, his defense is perhaps the right's strongest expression of support.[12]

2.2. LIBERAL PROCEDURALISM AND SPECIFIC GOODS

Apart from these three treatments, liberal egalitarians have almost entirely ignored the distribution of leisure, their engagement with the subject limited to only passing references. Though ultimately mistaken, the cursory attention the subject has received is not entirely unwarranted given how leisure has been standardly conceptualized. That is, leisure has been understood as a specific good, and on the liberal proceduralist approach to distributive justice, the distribution of such specific goods is presumptively not a proper object of concern. Thus, when leisure is understood in this way, theorists of distributive justice are prima facie not wrong to disregard leisure.

The liberal proceduralist approach to distributive justice derives from liberal egalitarianism's two central commitments: to both individual freedom of choice and some degree of equality in the distribution of society's benefits. If a society subscribed only to a liberal principle of justice, without any concern for realizing some degree of equality in the distribution of advantages either as individuals begin life or throughout their lives, given the inequalities in individual's talents, characters, and backgrounds, the distribution of benefits in the society predictably would be highly unequal. Conversely, if a society held only an egalitarian principle of justice, with no concern for respecting individual freedom, the most efficient and effective way to realize an equal distribution of benefits among the society's members likely would be to centrally distribute shares irrespective of individuals'

---

12 Jeremy Waldron, *Liberal Rights: Collected Papers, 1981–1991* (Cambridge: Cambridge University Press, 1993), 13. See also Charles R. Beitz, *The Idea of Human Rights* (Oxford: Oxford University Press, 2009), 61; James Griffin, *On Human Rights* (Oxford: Oxford University Press, 2008), 16, 180; David L. Richards and Benjamin C. Carbonetti, "Worth What We Decide: A Defense of the Right to Leisure," *International Journal of Human Rights* 17 (2013): 329–49; Risse, "A Right to Work?," 34; Mathias Risse, *On Global Justice* (Princeton: Princeton University Press, 2012), 245–60.

choices. The basic solution to resolving this central tension is liberal proceduralism.

Liberal proceduralism is best understood in contrast to its alternative, which, following the economist James Tobin, can be labeled "specific egalitarianism."[13] Say a society has a highly unequal distribution of food, with some people having an abundance and others having little. The specific egalitarian response to this inequality in food among the society's members is to redistribute food so that all have the same amount or, more plausibly, that all have enough. The specific egalitarian would achieve this result by directly altering the distribution of food, either by distributing food through public kitchens or pantries or by distributing food stamps. The liberal proceduralist, by contrast, would respond to the inequality in the distribution of food by examining the underlying distribution of income and wealth in the society. If the unequal distribution of food results from an inequality in the distribution of income and wealth, the liberal proceduralist response is to remedy that objectionable inequality in income and wealth through general taxation and transfer measures rather than to directly address the inequality in the distribution of food. If instead the unequal distribution of food does not result from any objectionable inequality in the distribution of income and wealth (but rather, say, from differences in individuals' preferences), the liberal proceduralist will be untroubled by that inequality. Thus, whereas the specific egalitarian is primarily concerned with inequalities in specific goods and aims to redress those inequalities directly, the general egalitarian is primarily concerned with inequalities in resources (like income and wealth) and seeks to remedy those inequalities in resources rather than in specific goods.

The liberal proceduralist approach is illustrated by an example drawn from Ronald Dworkin's theory of "equality of resources." Imagine that a number of shipwreck survivors wash ashore on a deserted island rich in natural resources.[14] The castaways are all equally talented and endowed—equal in strength, intelligence, skills, perseverance, attentiveness, and so on. Faced

13 Tobin labels liberal proceduralism "general egalitarianism." Tobin, "On Limiting the Domain of Inequality," *Journal of Law and Economics* 13 (1970): 263–77. For a discussion of general and specific egalitarianism, see Debra Satz, *Why Some Things Should Not Be For Sale: The Moral Limits of Markets* (Oxford: Oxford University Press, 2010), 76–84.

14 The island example is a simplified version of the one Dworkin employs in "Equality of Resources" (1981) in *Sovereign Virtue: The Theory and Practice of Equality* (Cambridge, MA: Harvard University Press, 2000).

with the prospect of how to divide up the natural resources of the island among themselves, the new immigrants (for rescue is unlikely) decide to divide the resources equally since none has any prior claim. To divide the island's resources equally, the immigrants distribute among themselves an equal number of clamshells to each and then hold an auction for different plots of land. Though the immigrants are equally talented, they nonetheless have different preferences, and they use their clamshells to select different plots of land in accordance with their preferences: some select smaller, beachfront plots and others larger, inland plots; some select remote, fertile plots and others central, rocky plots; and so on. With the different plots thusly distributed, the immigrants then decide to use them differently: some choose to work long hours fishing or gardening while others choose to spend most of their hours swimming or sunbathing; one with a flat plot erects a tennis court, another with a central plot makes a kitchen, and a third with a wooded plot builds furniture; and so forth. The immigrants, retaining their clamshell currency, then trade with each other for the various products and services they each can provide. After the initial auction and their different choices and trades, the immigrants' lives all look rather different: some have few possessions but a great deal of rest and relaxation, while others have abundant possessions but a great deal of long and hard work. Though the castaways began with equal shares of "resources" (both talents and clamshells), after a period of time they end up with different bundles of "specific goods" (both possessions and lifestyles). According to Dworkin's theory of equality of resources, given these facts alone, the resulting distribution of specific goods on the island is just.

Different theories might instead find the distribution on the island unjust, on the basis of these or additional facts, and especially once one adds the inevitabilities of illness, children, natural disasters, and so forth, and accordingly prescribe some later redistribution of clamshells. Nonetheless, Dworkin's island story provides a clear example of the liberal proceduralist approach to distributive justice: rather than focus on and directly intervene in the distribution of specific goods, the liberal proceduralist targets the distribution of resources and leaves the distribution of specific goods to individual choices mediated through market mechanisms.

Dworkin's island example also provides a basis for drawing a more careful distinction between the categories of "resources" and "specific goods".[15]

---

15 The distinction between resources and specific goods fits most readily with a "resourcist" theory of distributive justice—that is, one that uses resources themselves as the metric

Resources are the "inputs" that are generally necessary to pursue one's conception of the good, whatever it may be. (I use conception of the good in the broad sense of a plan of life, idea of the good life, or even preferred lifestyle.[16]) Resources may be divided into various subcategories, including material resources (e.g., money or property), personal resources (e.g., intelligence, strength, or a work ethic), and "opportunity" resources (that is, the legal rights and protections or social conditions that allow one to pursue one's conception of the good, e.g., freedom of movement or a functioning labor market).

Specific goods are the particular components that are part of one's particular conception of the good. Specific goods too can be divided into subcategories, including material goods (e.g., food, a plot of land, a tennis racket), "experiential" goods (e.g., tennis playing, friendship), and "social" goods (e.g., public parks, a community of tennis players). The use of "goods" does not, accordingly, refer strictly to goods as material commodities, as things of value, or as privately held entities, but more broadly to any particular object or experience that contributes to or constitutes one's particular conception of the good. To take an example, if one's conception of the good involves bicycling,

---

for assessing individuals' distributive shares. Other theories use different metrics, but nonetheless still rely on the distinction between resources and specific goods; they simply use different metrics to assess individuals' distributive shares. A theory that, for instance, uses capabilities as the relevant metric focuses on individuals' capabilities to function as democratic citizens as the relevant point of distributive concern, but these capabilities are themselves determined by the resources individuals possess or can access, and unjust distributions of capabilities are addressed by distributing or otherwise providing individuals with the required resources. The same pattern holds for Richard Arneson's metric of opportunity for welfare and G. A. Cohen's metric of access to advantage. See Elizabeth Anderson, "What Is the Point of Equality?" *Ethics* 109 (1999): 287–337 and "Justifying the Capabilities Approach to Justice," in *Measuring Justice: Primary Goods and Capabilities*, ed. Harry Brighouse and Ingrid Robeyns (Cambridge: Cambridge University Press, 2010), 81–101; Arneson, "Equality and Equal Opportunity for Welfare," *Philosophical Studies* 56 (1989): 77–93 and "Equality of Opportunity for Welfare Defended and Recanted," *Journal of Political Philosophy* 7 (1999): 488–97; and Cohen, "On the Currency of Egalitarian Justice," in G.A. Cohen, *On the Currency of Egalitarian Justice, and Other Essays in Political Philosophy*, ed. Michael Otsuka. (Princeton: Princeton University Press, 2011), 3–43. The theories of distributive justice to which this distinction does not readily apply are those that do not follow the standard liberal proceduralist approach.

16 Though some of these terms suggest that one's conception of the good must depend on a rational or coherent plan, or a "unified conception of one's overall purposes," my use of the term does not depend on it having this strong meaning. For a discussion of this point, see Charles Larmore, "The Idea of a Life Plan," *Social Philosophy and Policy* 16 (1999): 96–112.

then time spent bicycling, access to a bicycle, and bicycle lanes might be the specific goods that are part of one's conception of the good, whereas money to buy a bicycle, freedom of movement, and functioning commodity markets might be the resources that are necessary to pursue one's conception of the good.

Note that the distinction between specific goods and resources is not that the latter are instrumental to pursuing one's conception of the good, whereas the former are intrinsic to one's conception of the good. Resources are instrumental to the pursuit of one's conception of the good, but so too may specific goods be: as in the example, both freedom of movement and bicycle lanes are instrumental to the pursuit of one's conception of the good, though the former is a resource and the latter a specific good. Instead, the relevant distinction is that specific goods are the *particular* goods that one requires to pursue one's *particular* conception of the good, whereas resources are the *all-purpose* means that one generally requires to pursue one's conception of the good, *whatever it may be*. Unless one's particular plan of life involves bicycling, bicycle lanes are generally not instrumental to the pursuit of one's conception of the good, whereas freedom of movement is generally instrumental to the pursuit of one's conception of the good, whatever it may be. It must also be noted that the boundaries between resources and specific goods are not always sharply defined. If, for instance, bicycling were the predominant mode of transport in a given society, bicycle lanes might be more properly regarded as resources.

The liberal proceduralist approach to distributive justice is, then, to redress inequalities by focusing on the background distribution of resources rather than the resulting distribution of specific goods. Liberal proceduralism is justified broadly on the values of individual freedom of choice and personal autonomy. By providing individuals with the resources they require to pursue their conceptions of the good, whatever they are, rather than with the specific goods that are necessary to pursue only some conceptions of the good, the state gives individuals wider latitude to direct and lead their own lives as they see fit. More specifically, the liberal values of individual freedom and personal autonomy ground three distinct principles—the principle of anti-paternalism, the principle of non-perfectionism, and the principle of neutrality—each of which provides reason to favor liberal proceduralism over specific egalitarianism. Though the values of individual freedom and personal autonomy do not necessarily justify these three principles, and though these three principles do not necessarily dictate liberal proceduralism, nonetheless these liberal values and the three principles do standardly support general over specific egalitarianism.[17]

The liberal commitment to individual freedom, specifically to respect an individual's judgment over how to conduct her own life and affairs, grounds a principle of anti-paternalism. Following judgment-based definitions of paternalism, a state action is paternalistic when it is justified by the view that the state's judgment about how one should run one's life is superior to one's own judgment.[18] According to the principle of anti-paternalism, a state action with a paternalist motive or justification is presumptively impermissible. The justification of particular instances of specific egalitarianism need not be paternalist: for instance, if the only way for the state to solve a collective action problem is to provide a specific good (e.g., open green space) directly, rather than by providing all citizens with the all-purpose resources to procure that specific good, the justification for the state's action is not paternalist. Nonetheless, the justification of specific egalitarianism does often depend on paternalistic motives, as, for instance, when the state provides the hungry with food stamps rather than with money to purchase food because it believes its judgment is (or is likely to be) better than the recipient's judgment about how best to spend the money. More important, liberal proceduralism necessarily involves the state *not* substituting its superior judgment for an

17 An additional reason to favor liberal proceduralism is that it is often more efficient than specific egalitarianism. If efficiency is defined in terms of Pareto improvements, so that one state of affairs is more efficient than another if it improves the positions of some without making anyone else worse off, general egalitarianism often will be more efficient than specific egalitarianism in two ways. First, say someone who has little food is granted a food stamp, but that she would prefer to use the equivalent value of the food stamp on building a monument to her god (as in T. M. Scanlon's classic example): giving her the equivalent value rather than the food stamp is more efficient in that it makes her better off without making anyone else worse off. Second, say she decides to trade her food stamp with someone else for its market value in money, thereby adding unnecessary transactions and their attendant costs to the market: again, giving her the equivalent value rather than the food stamp is more efficient in that it makes her and everyone else better off without making anyone worse off (assuming in both cases that no one is made worse off by having their preference to give food stamps rather than money unmet). Though the argument for liberal proceduralism from efficiency may carry some weight in a liberal theory of justice, it is the anti-paternalist, non-perfectionist, and neutrality principles that provide first-order reasons in favor of general egalitarianism. Scanlon, "Preferences and Urgency," in *The Difficulty of Tolerance: Essays in Political Philosophy*, 70–83. (Cambridge: Cambridge University Press, 2003).

18 Seana Valentine Shiffrin, "Paternalism, Unconscionability Doctrine, and Accommodation," *Philosophy & Public Affairs* 29 (2000): 218; Jonathan Quong, *Liberalism without Perfection* (Oxford: Oxford University Press, 2010), 80.

individual's own judgment about how to conduct her own affairs. Thus, the principle of anti-paternalism provides a presumptive reason to favor the liberal proceduralist approach to distributive justice.

The same commitment to respecting an individual's own judgment about how best to live his life also grounds a principle of non-perfectionism. Perfectionist state actions encourage citizens to pursue ways of life that the state holds to be valuable or good, or, alternately, discourage citizens from pursuing ways of life that are held to be worthless or bad.[19] The principle of non-perfectionism holds that state actions that are justified on the basis of perfectionist considerations (that is, judgments about better or worse ways of life) are impermissible. Again, often instances of specific egalitarianism are justified on perfectionist grounds, as, for instance, when the state provides individuals with access to the fine arts because it holds that a life that includes the fine arts is better than one that does not. (Though, again too, instances of specific egalitarianism that could be justified on perfectionist grounds need not in fact be perfectionist if they are justified on other grounds, as, for example, if the fine arts are subsidized as part of a broad public works program to counter unemployment.) Though some instances of specific egalitarianism may be proscribed by the principle of non-perfectionism, more significantly, the liberal proceduralist approach is necessarily *not* perfectionist. If the state provides one with all-purpose resources that one can use to pursue any conception of the good, without any concern for the value of the conception of the good that one might hold, the state is not acting on the basis of perfectionist considerations.[20] Again then, the principle of non-perfectionism provides a presumptive reason in favor of liberal proceduralism.

Third, and finally, the liberal value of personal autonomy grounds a principle of neutrality. The state acts non-neutrally, following the conception of neutrality of treatment, when it acts in a way that is more accommodating to some conceptions of the good than others, to the effect that individuals with the disadvantaged conceptions of the good are denied the same

---

19 Joseph Raz, *The Morality of Freedom* (Oxford: Clarendon Press, 1986), 133.

20 Indeed, a test of whether something is a resource or a specific good is whether providing the thing in question favors a particular view of the good life or a particular way of living. Thus, when one criticizes Rawls's primary good of income and wealth as favoring materialistic ways of life, the appropriate liberal proceduralist defense is to show that income and wealth are valuable whatever one's conception of the good (and thereby a resource and not a specific good). For such critiques, see Adina Schwartz, "Moral Neutrality and Primary Goods," *Ethics* 83 (1973): 294–307 and Michael Teitelman, "The Limits of Individualism," *Journal of Philosophy* 69 (1972): 545–56. For such a defense, see Freeman, *Rawls*, 152–54.

opportunities that individuals with the advantaged conceptions of the good enjoy, all else equal, to pursue their values and commitments. The principle of neutrality requires that the state not act in such a way that is more or less accommodating of some conceptions of the good than others. The state, on this view, does not violate the principle of neutrality when it provides equal "inputs" (rules, mechanisms, resources, or goods) for all conceptions of the good, by enforcing a set of general rules, by providing resources that contribute to all or almost all conceptions of the good, or by providing different specific goods for different conceptions of the good in an evenhanded way.[21]

Though it is in principle possible to achieve neutrality of treatment by providing different specific goods for different conceptions of the good in equal measure (and though it may be necessary to achieve neutrality in this way in some instances), specific egalitarianism is, in practice and in general, the most difficult way to satisfy neutrality of treatment. It requires the state to assess the range of contending conceptions of the good, to then determine which goods to provide, and finally to assess how to provide those goods in an evenhanded way, a task that may in some cases be practically impossible. Instead, the other two ways of achieving neutrality of treatment—enforcing a set of general rules or providing resources that are valuable to all or nearly all conceptions of the good—are both, when available, more straightforward ways to satisfy neutrality and both are forms of liberal proceduralism. Thus, the principle of neutrality, too, provides a presumptive reason to favor the liberal proceduralist approach to distributive justice.

Though it is possible to override the presumptive case in favor of liberal proceduralism, grounded in the principles of anti-paternalism, non-perfectionism, and neutrality, by providing a special justification for a given specific good, the default approach is to address the distribution of all-

---

21 Alan Patten, "Liberal Neutrality: A Reinterpretation and Defense," *Journal of Political Philosophy* 20 (2011): 249–72. Neutrality of treatment is to be distinguished from its primary rivals, neutrality of intentions (or aims or justifications) and neutrality of effects (or outcomes). Neutrality of intentions is violated if the state adopts a policy with the aim of favoring a particular conception of the good or with a justification that involves valuing a particular conception of the good over others. Neutrality of effects is violated if the state adopts a policy that has the effect of making a particular conception of the good more successful than others. Because neutrality of intentions is, in the relevant respects, indistinguishable from the principle of non-perfectionism, and because neutrality of effects has similar implications but is widely rejected as too strong a requirement, I focus instead on neutrality of treatment.

purpose resources rather than the distribution of specific goods. Because, as I will now show, leisure has been standardly understood as a specific good rather than as a resource, it is therefore not surprising that leisure has generally been neglected by liberal theories of justice.

2.3 LEISURE AS A SPECIFIC GOOD

There are, broadly stated, three ways that leisure has standardly been conceptualized by political philosophers, and on each conception leisure is a specific good: leisure as time engaged in contemplation, leisure as time engaged in recreational activities, and leisure as time not engaged in paid work.

Leisure as Time Engaged in Contemplation

Though the latter two conceptions are the more common understandings today, the first—Aristotle's classical conception of leisure as contemplation—is the most philosophically sophisticated.[22] Aristotle conceives of leisure (*schole*) as activities that are done "for their own sake"—the intrinsically valuable pursuits in which one finds human excellence and happiness.[23] He identifies as not leisure (*ascholia*) all those things that are done "for the sake of other things," because they are "deemed necessary" for instrumental reasons. The activities Aristotle describes as not leisure, as they are done for the sake of instrumental reasons, can be put into three categories. First, those activities that are done for man's material sustenance and comfort, to satisfy the "necessaries of life," like work and business, are not leisure. In a phrase Aristotle repeats, just as war must be "for the sake of peace," so "business [must be] for

---

22 For contemporary accounts informed by Aristotle's account of leisure, see Josef Pieper, *Leisure, the Basis of Culture*, trans. Alexander Dru (New York: Pantheon Books, 1952); Sebastian De Grazia, *Of Time, Work, and Leisure* (1962; repr., New York: Vintage, 1994); and, more recently, Robert Skidelsky and Edward Skidelsky, *How Much Is Enough? Money and the Good Life* (New York: Other Press, 2012), 165–67.

23 Strictly speaking, Aristotle defines leisure as intrinsically valuable activities themselves, not the time in which one does such activities. This distinction is not significant for the present treatment, so, for the sake of consistency, I refer to the Aristotelian conception as the time when one is engaged in intrinsically valuable activities.

the sake of leisure."[24] Second, play, recreation, and other amusements are not leisure, for if play were leisure, "then play would be the end of life." Instead, play is done to relieve the toil of work: "he who is hard at work has need of relaxation, and play gives relaxation." Play and other "amusements" are, in this way, like "medicines" to obtain "rest" and "relaxation."[25] Third, the activities of politics and ruling are not strictly leisure because they are necessary as a means to attain happiness for one's city, and not an end in themselves.[26] Though citizens require leisure, politics itself is not properly a leisure activity.[27]

The activities associated with leisure include, in the strictest sense, only philosophical contemplation—the "activity of study" which "aims at no end apart from itself." Aristotle does, however, also permit that music, properly undertaken, can be leisurely, so long as it is not done primarily "for the sake of pleasure" but instead for "intellectual enjoyment." Broadening the range of leisure activities from only philosophy to also include music allows for leisure to be something that all citizens could enjoy.[28]

Aristotle's conception of leisure (and its neo-Aristotelian interpretations) must be categorized as a specific good. Because Aristotle's conception associates leisure with particular activities, like philosophical contemplation or music, that are identified as intrinsically valuable by a perfectionist theory of human excellence, it describes leisure in such a way that it is properly regarded as a particular component of a particular conception of the good.

24 Aristotle, *The Politics*, in *The Politics and Constitution of Athens*, ed. Stephen Everson (Cambridge: Cambridge University Press, 1996), 1333a29–1333b1, 1334a12–39, 1337b27–1338a14.

25 *Politics*, 1337b34–42; Aristotle, *Nicomachean Ethics*, trans. and ed. Terence Irwin (Indianapolis: Hackett, 1999), 1176b7–1177a1. See Joseph Owens, "Aristotle on Leisure," *Canadian Journal of Philosophy* 11 (1981): 717.

26 "The actions of the politician . . . deny us leisure." *Nicomachean Ethics*, 1177b13. For this position, see Carnes Lord, *Education and Culture in the Political Thought of Aristotle* (Ithaca: Cornell University Press, 1982). Whether or not politics qualifies as intrinsically good and so as a leisure activity is disputed, as this question is part of a broader unresolved dispute about whether the life of the statesman is a good life or whether it is in conflict with the contemplative life. For the contrary position on politics as leisure, see, for instance, David J. Depew, "Politics, Music, and Contemplation in Aristotle's Ideal State," in *A Companion to Aristotle's Politics*, ed. David Keyt and Fred D. Miller, Jr. (Oxford: Blackwell, 1991), 346–80.

27 *Politics*, 1277b34–1278a23, 1328b40–1329a2.

28 *Nicomachean Ethics*, 1177b21; *Politics*, 1337b27–1338a23. See also Friedrich Solmsen, "Leisure and Play in Aristotle's Ideal State," *Rheinisches Museum für Philologie* 107 (1964): 217–18 and Richard Kraut, *Aristotle: Political Philosophy* (Oxford: Oxford University Press, 2002), 197–201.

Leisure as Time Engaged in Recreational Activities

The second standard conception of leisure—leisure as time engaged in recreational activities—accords much more closely with contemporary usage, but has also received much less sustained development by political philosophers. On this view, leisure is the time when one is engaged in "recreational" activities, defined broadly as activities that are typically pursued in one's society for the sake of entertainment, enjoyment, or relaxation, often denoted by the appendage of "for pleasure," as in "reading for pleasure." This conception of leisure—more often employed by sociologists and historians—is occasionally suggested by theorists of distributive justice with references to "leisure activities" and "leisure pursuits."[29] Its most notable articulation is in Martha Nussbaum's list of central human capabilities as the capability of "play," defined as "being able to laugh, to play, to enjoy recreational activities."[30]

Though not necessarily wedded to a particular theory of human excellence like Aristotle's conception of leisure, leisure as time engaged in recreational activities is, on the liberal proceduralist approach, still appropriately identified as a specific good. Time engaged in recreational activities is a particular component of some people's particular conceptions of the good but not others', and people prefer to spend more or less time engaged in such activities. On Nussbaum's capabilities theory, the state ought to provide only the capability (that is, the opportunity) to engage in recreational activities, and not directly provide or promote time engaged in recreational activities. Accordingly, Nussbaum clarifies that "a person who has opportunities for play can always choose a workaholic life."[31] Yet, on the liberal proceduralist approach, it is unwarranted for the state to promote the capability to engage in this *particular* functioning, rather than the capability, more generally, to pursue one's conception of the good, whatever it is.[32]

---

29 Anderson, "What Is the Point of Equality?," 322; G. A. Cohen, *Rescuing Justice and Equality* (Cambridge, MA: Harvard University Press, 2008), 212.

30 Martha C. Nussbaum, *Women and Human Development: The Capabilities Approach* (Cambridge: Cambridge University Press, 2000), 78–80.

31 Ibid., 87.

32 For this reason, Nussbaum's version of a capabilities theory does not fit squarely within the standard liberal proceduralist approach. Nussbaum argues that her approach is "very close" to Rawls's use of primary goods, with the main difference being that her list of capabilities is longer and more definite than Rawls's list of primary goods. Yet, Rawls's list of primary goods is a set of all-purpose resources generally required for the functioning of citizens,

For the state to provide or otherwise promote time engaged in recreational activities is, absent an intervening justification, to violate the nonperfectionist, anti-paternalist, and neutrality principles. While it may be easier to provide an overriding justification for this conception of leisure than for Aristotle's (on, for instance, the grounds of providing public goods), leisure understood as time engaged in recreational activities is nonetheless a specific good that, on the liberal proceduralist approach, presumptively ought to be distributed in accordance with the individual choices of citizens equipped with the necessary all-purpose resources to pursue such activities.[33]

Leisure as Time Not Engaged in Paid Work

Of the three standard conceptions of leisure, by far the most common within liberal theories of justice is time not engaged in paid work. This is the conception employed both by Dworkin and Rawls, and other theorists, following in their steps, have almost universally adopted their conception of leisure as time not engaged in paid work. Given that Dworkin's theory of distributive justice takes a stylized market as its foundation and that it was an economist who first pressed Rawls to address leisure, it is perhaps not surprising that their conception of leisure—and thereby that of liberal theorists of justice generally—follows the textbook economic definition and model of leisure.

On the simple neoclassical model of the labor market, leisure is defined as all time when one is not engaged in income-earning market work.[34] Leisure,

---

whereas Nussbaum's list of capabilities instead specifies a list of particular functionings. See Nussbaum, *Women and Human Development*, 88–89 for the argument about the similarity between her and Rawls's approaches, and Rawls, *Justice as Fairness*, 168–73 for his treatment of capabilities, and Rawls, "Social Unity and Primary Goods," in *John Rawls: Collected Papers*, ed. Samuel Freeman (Cambridge, MA: Harvard University Press, 1999), 359–87 for a discussion of how primary goods are the "necessary conditions for realizing the powers of moral personality and are all-purpose means for a sufficiently wide range of final ends" (367).

33 For a discussion of the public goods argument, see, for instance, Harry Brighouse, "Neutrality, Publicity, and State Funding of the Arts," *Philosophy & Public Affairs* 24 (1995): 35–63, and Ronald Dworkin, "Can a Liberal State Support Art?," in *A Matter of Principle* (Cambridge, MA: Harvard University Press, 1985), 221–33.

34 It is important to note that this model of the labor market is indeed the simple textbook model and that, as such, it lacks the complexity and qualifications of more sophisticated models of work hours employed by labor economists. Because some of the theoretical and empirical deviations from the simple neoclassical textbook model are significant to my argu-

on this view, is defined strictly in opposition to paid work: whereas market work is income-earning, leisure is income-consuming, either directly (through income expenditure) or indirectly (through the opportunity cost of forgone income). According to the textbook model of "labor-leisure choice," individual workers choose to allot their time to either paid work or to leisure in accordance with their preferences, specifically in accordance with their preferences for the intrinsic and extrinsic benefits of work relative to those of leisure. As individuals with diverse tastes and circumstances, individual workers (or potential workers) have different preferences for how much time they wish to spend engaged in paid work relative to leisure, and they select their hours of paid work in accordance with their diverse income-leisure preferences. In short, individual workers face a "trade-off between work and leisure," and can, in accordance with their preferences, choose to spend a given period of time to earn income through paid work or to forgo additional income and "purchase" or "consume" leisure.[35]

Most liberal theorists adopt this standard economic model of leisure in two important respects. First, most basically, they conceive of leisure on the economic terms as time not engaged in paid work.[36] Second, and just as significantly, they follow the textbook model's treatment of leisure as a good

---

ment, I discuss some of the features of the more sophisticated labor market models in Chapter 4. Here, however, the simple model is sufficient, for it is this textbook model that liberal theorists have employed in their treatments of leisure. For an illuminating (and, to the best of my knowledge, the only comprehensive) history of economic models of leisure, see John Alsworth Menefee, "The Economics of Leisure: The Evolution of the Labor-Leisure Tradeoff in Economic Doctrines" (PhD diss., Duke University, 1974).

35 George Borjas, *Labor Economics*, 7th ed. (New York: McGraw-Hill, 2016), 21–49; N. Gregory Mankiw, *Principles of Economics*, 7th ed. (Stamford, CT: Cengage Learning, 2015), 380.

36 See, for example, Joseph H. Carens, *Equality, Moral Incentives, and the Market: An Essay in Utopian Politico-Economic Theory* (Chicago: University of Chicago Press, 1981), 50, 147; Cohen, *Rescuing Justice and Equality*, 105, 211; Miriam Cohen Christofidis, "Talent, Slavery, and Envy," in *Dworkin and His Critics: with Replies by Dworkin*, ed. Justine Burley (Malden, MA: Blackwell, 2004), 34; Dworkin, *Sovereign Virtue*, 329; Marc Fleurbaey, *Fairness, Responsibility, and Welfare* (Oxford: Oxford University Press, 2008), 101; Michael Otsuka, "Liberty, Equality, Envy, and Abstraction," in Burley, *Dworkin and His Critics*, 71; Eric Rakowski, *Equal Justice* (Oxford: Clarendon Press, 1991), 107–19; Stuart White, "The Egalitarian Earnings Subsidy Scheme," *British Journal of Political Science* 29 (1999): 604ff.; Philippe Van Parijs, "Equality of Resources versus Undominated Diversity," in Burley, *Dworkin and His Critics*, 45; and Van Parijs, *Real Freedom for All*, 196.

that individuals can "purchase" or not, and in varying quantities, in accordance with their preferences. Nearly every reference to leisure in liberal theories of justice is in the context of discussions of citizens' "income/leisure preferences" or their preferences with respect to "income-leisure trade-offs." Dworkin refers to citizens' decisions to "consume leisure" or to "purchase leisure," and G. A. Cohen suggests that "we could think of income and leisure on the model of apples and oranges."[37]

This second point of congruence between the textbook economic model and the usual liberal conception of leisure is particularly noteworthy because it explicitly highlights how leisure is regarded on this view as a specific good. How much leisure one enjoys is a particular component of one's particular conception of the good, and leisure is, as such, a specific good that one can choose in accordance with one's preferences. Different conceptions of the good include different amounts of leisure: one might be a leisure lover or a work lover, or, as Dworkin more pointedly expresses it, an "ant" or a "grasshopper." Though it may be relevant whether one chooses leisure over paid work in determining what one's fair claim to resources is (as in Rawls's discussion of leisure), for the state to be concerned with providing or promoting leisure, in itself, is contrary to the non-perfectionist, antipaternalist, and neutrality principles, for leisure is a specific good that is of varying importance to different conceptions of the good. Indeed, the argument that would, in practice, most readily provide citizens with opportunities for leisure—Philippe Van Parijs's argument for an unconditional basic income—in fact relies on the premise that the state ought to be neutral between leisure-loving and work-loving conceptions of the good.[38]

2.4 FROM LEISURE TO FREE TIME

As these various conceptions show, leisure has been defined both negatively, as the time when one is not engaged in particular activities, and positively, as the time when one is engaged in other activities. Moreover, the par-

---

37 Van Parijs, *Real Freedom for All*, 61; Dworkin, *Sovereign Virtue*, 89, 90; Cohen, *Rescuing Justice and Equality*, 110n53.

38 Van Parijs, *Real Freedom for All*, 89; Dworkin, *Sovereign Virtue*, 329; Van Parijs, "Why Surfers Should Be Fed," 102, 111–12. For a discussion of the Van Parijs neutrality argument for the basic income, see Simon Birnbaum, "Should Surfers Be Ostracized? Basic Income, Liberal Neutrality, and the Work Ethos," *Philosophy, Politics & Economics* 10 (2011): 396–419.

ticular activities that leisure has been associated with, either as the synonym or the antonym—paid work, play, and philosophical contemplation—seem to exist on entirely different registers. Yet, despite the diversity of the existing conceptions and their apparent dissimilarities, a feature that unites them all is the opposition to some idea of necessity. On each of these conceptions, leisure is the time when one is not engaged in activities because one *must* or *has to*, but instead because one *can* or *wants to*.

Part of what distinguishes paid work, for instance, from leisure is that paid work is an activity that one must do in order to earn a living, whereas leisure is the time when one can engage in other pursuits. Similarly, part of what associates leisure with recreation is that recreational activities are those one chooses to do because one wants to do them, not because one has to. When we think of the professional movie critic at the cinema on assignment, this otherwise paradigmatic recreational activity—going to the movies—does not seem so leisurely. Even the Aristotelian conception of leisure as philosophical contemplation depends on this dichotomy: leisure is associated with contemplation because it is done for its own sake, unlike those activities that are done because they are instrumentally necessary to one's ends.

To be sure, on almost all conceptions, leisure may be distinguished from its opposite by additional features as well. Paid work, for instance, might be further distinguished from leisure because paid work, unlike leisure, is performed under the thumb of another. Or, in the same way, perhaps recreational activities qualify as leisure not only because one wants to do them, but also because one does them with pleasure. Still, across all existing conceptions, leisure is in some way defined in opposition to necessity. Certainly, too, the operational idea of necessity varies across conceptions: the reason paid work is necessary is not the same as the reasons why play or contemplation are not. Nonetheless, the common core of the concept is its opposition to necessity.

In Chapter 3, I show that, apart from the various ways that leisure has been understood as a specific good, it is also possible to reconceptualize leisure as a resource—as the resource of free time. Putting the antithesis to necessity at the core, I argue on behalf of recognizing free time, defined as time that is not committed to meeting one's own or one's dependents' basic needs, as a resource, for citizens require such time to pursue their conceptions of the good, whatever they may be.

Before turning to the task of reconceptualizing leisure as a resource in Chapter 3, it is worth emphasizing that the standard liberal egalitarian approach holds only that, *absent some special intervening justification*, the state ought to address the distribution of resources rather than specific goods. That is, the standard liberal egalitarian approach provides only a *presumptive* position in favor of general over specific egalitarianism. This presumptive case could be defeated for a given specific good by providing an argument about why the distribution of that particular specific good ought to be addressed directly. The types of special justifications that could be offered are myriad: there are possible arguments from, at least, collective action, efficiency, social equality, vulnerability, and exploitation.

It is not my aim to reject the possibility of providing special justifications of this type to establish that theories of distributive justice ought to address the distribution of leisure as a specific good. There are many legitimate reasons why theories of distributive justice may be concerned with the distribution of leisure, even as a specific good. Arguments for maximum hours laws, for instance—one of the most powerful ways to affect the distribution of leisure—can and have been defended on the grounds that they reduce unemployment, protect workers from coercion, preserve family life, and are a warranted case of paternalism to preserve the health of workers. While I do not necessarily endorse such arguments, I also do not reject them: they are simply alternative strategies not pursued here.

Instead, my aim is to provide a more fundamental argument for why free time must be incorporated into a theory of distributive justice. If free time is reconceptualized as a resource, not only *can* one argue, if some special justification applies, that theories of justice ought to address free time, but instead one *must* accept, unless there is some argument to the contrary, that our theories of justice must address free time. By demonstrating how leisure can be reconceptualized from a specific good to the resource of free time, my approach provides a more comprehensive and fundamental case for recognizing free time as a distinct object of distributive justice.

CHAPTER 3

FREE TIME AS A RESOURCE

Leisure—conceptualized as time not engaged in paid work, or as time devoted to play, or as time spent in philosophical contemplation—has standardly been understood within political philosophy in general, and liberal egalitarianism in particular, as a specific good: a particular component of particular conceptions of the good. As such, it has been regarded as not an appropriate object of distributive concern. Yet, though leisure has standardly been understood as a specific good, it is also possible, while retaining the core of the concept, its opposition to necessity, to reconceive of it as the resource of free time. Distributive justice requires that citizens have their fair share of resources, with which citizens can then pursue their preferred bundles of specific goods, like leisure, in accordance with their own understandings of the good life. Thus, when free time is rightly recognized as a resource, its place in liberal theory is reversed, moving it from a peripheral to central concern.

Leisure can be understood not only as time engaged or not engaged in specific activities, but as time when one can engage in any activity of one's choosing. From the Latin root *licere*, meaning "to be permitted," leisure can be understood as time that is free—time that one can devote, at one's discretion, to one's chosen ends. The opposite is time constrained by necessity, time that one must devote to particular ends. So described, it is apparent how free time could plausibly be understood as a resource. The idea is a familiar one: we commonly think of free time as time that is "one's own," when one can do what one wants, when one can do as one chooses. Yet this familiar idea, when pushed, is vague and underspecified. What marks a period of time as free or necessary? Is free time simply the time not engaged in a set of typically necessary activities, like paid work or household chores? Does it matter whether one judges or experiences the time spent as necessary or discretionary? What if one does not "really need" to do some task or does it "only because one wants to"? Is there a way of objectively distinguishing free from necessary time?

As these questions indicate, just as there are multiple ways of understanding leisure, so are there multiple ways of defining free time. Though the core of the concept is its contrast with necessity, there is no single "true" conception of leisure or free time; which conception is appropriate depends on its context and purpose. The task here is to develop more precisely the familiar idea—that free time is time that one can devote, at one's discretion, to one's own chosen ends—in such a way that free time is appropriately understood as a resource to which citizens could plausibly have claims in a public and feasible liberal egalitarian theory of justice.

I will argue that free time, defined as the time not committed to meeting one's own, or one's dependents', basic needs, is such a resource. I begin by developing the intuitive case for recognizing free time, understood in this way, as such a resource. I will then more precisely present the criteria for an object to be a resource in a public and feasible theory of justice, before canvassing three ways, drawn from time-use research, of defining free time. I argue that the typically necessary and subjectively necessary definitions of free time are not appropriately understood as resources in the relevant sense, and instead argue for a particular objective definition of free time, which I develop in the final sections.

3.2 THE RESOURCE OF TIME

To develop the idea of free time as a resource, it is helpful to begin with the recognition that *time itself* is a resource. This observation is commonly made by economists, for time, like capital, is one of the necessary inputs into any production function. Moreover, time, like other economic resources, is scarce; indeed, it is perhaps "the ultimate scarce resource."[1] But time is a

1 Clifford Sharp, *The Economics of Time* (New York: Wiley, 1981), 18.

necessary input not only for economic production, but also for any human action. No matter what one wishes to do, that action unavoidably requires time.[2] When one thinks of time, full stop, as a resource, the distribution of time need not be a concern for a theory of justice for it is, effectively, a problem solved: though some live longer than others, everyone automatically and necessarily possesses the same amount of time in a given period.[3] Everyone has only twenty-four hours in a day.

Though time, full stop, is appropriately described as a resource, this capacious understanding of time is not the only way to view time as a resource. Instead, one can identify a further temporal resource, free time: the time beyond that which one must devote to meeting one's own, or one's dependents', basic needs. In order to pursue a wide range of individual ends, to pursue one's conception of the good whatever it may be, one generally requires free time.

Consider two individuals who are identical in every respect except that one is able to earn at most five dollars per hour and the other twenty-five dollars per hour. Say that in order to get by in the society in which they live, in order to function at a basic level, a person must have an income of fifty dollars per day. The one who can earn only five dollars per hour accordingly has to work ten hours a day to earn the requisite income, while the one who can earn twenty-five dollars per hour has to work only two hours a day.[4] Though both have the same amount of time, full stop, they do not have the same amount of free time. The individual who must work only two hours a day to earn the requisite income has significantly more time available to her

2 In the words of Robert E. Goodin, James Mahmud Rice, Antti Parpo, and Lina Eriksson, "time is a necessary input into anything that one cares to do or to become," and as Todd D. Rakoff expresses the point, "time is a resource, a commodity to be directed to this use or that." Goodin et al., *Discretionary Time: A New Measure of Freedom* (Cambridge: Cambridge University Press, 2008), 4; Rakoff, *A Time for Every Purpose: Law and the Balance of Life* (Cambridge, MA: Harvard University Press, 2002). For an illuminating discussion of the ways in which time is like a natural resource, see D. G. Brown, "The Value of Time," *Ethics* 80 (1970): 173–84.

3 This is not to say that the length of average *lifetimes* could not be a legitimate distributive concern. Though the distribution of lifetime lengths is not usually addressed as a distributive concern *as such*, it is indirectly a concern in the distribution of health care and other life-preserving resources and goods.

4 Assume that one is able to find employment on terms that permit one to work only two hours per day. This condition often does not obtain, an important issue I will return to in 3.7 and 4.4.

to do all of the other things she might wish to do than the individual who has to work ten hours a day.

Though this example shows how paid work can subtract from one's free time, other activities can subtract from one's free time in precisely the same way. Indeed, one's free time is constrained not by engaging in a given *type* of activity, but by engaging in an activity that is *necessary* to function at a basic level in one's society, or to meet one's basic needs.[5] Just as it is generally necessary to engage in paid work in order to attain a socially and biologically determined level of basic functioning, it is also generally necessary to engage in some amount of household labor (cooking, cleaning, and the like), as well as some amount of personal care (eating, grooming, exercising, sleeping, and so forth). So long as it is *necessary* for one to do these activities to attain basic functioning, they detract from one's free time, for the time one must devote to them is not available for one to devote to other ends. Simply because one's time is spent engaged in an activity that is *typically* necessary does not entail that such time is not still free time. If one does not have to engage in a given activity to attain a basic level of functioning, but does so nonetheless, such time does not detract from one's free time, for it is still available to devote to any other end if one chooses.

To see this distinction, consider two individuals who spend all of their time engaged in the same types of activities for the same amounts of time: each spends twelve hours per day working for pay, eight hours sleeping, one hour eating, and so forth. The first is a wealthy heiress who could easily support herself with her investment income, though she actually chooses to spend a significant portion of her time working as a model. She is not contractually bound to work such long hours; every morning she receives a call from her agent asking if she would like to work that day and for how many hours, and she suffers no penalty if she chooses not to work. The second is a day laborer with no personal wealth who can command only low wages and so must work long hours to earn enough money just to get by. She is also

---

5 I here and throughout use the idea of functioning at a basic level—or "basic needs"—as it is commonly employed in the literature, that is as the demands that generally must be met for one to live at a minimally decent level in one's society. As Adam Smith expressed the idea, "By necessaries I understand not only the commodities which are indispensably necessary for the support of life, but whatever the custom of the country renders it indecent for creditable people, even the lowest order, to be without." Smith, *An Inquiry into the Nature and Causes of the Wealth of Nations* (1776; repr., Oxford: Oxford University Press, 1976), 869–70. See Amartya Sen, "Poor, Relatively Speaking," *Oxford Economic Papers* 35 (1983): 153–69.

not legally committed to working a certain number of hours: each day she is hired by a different person on an hourly basis for her day's work.

Though both the heiress and the day laborer engage in the same number of hours of paid work, it is implausible to contend that both thereby have the same amount of free time. They both can choose, strictly speaking, whether or not to work on a given day, but the heiress's paid work is discretionary in a way that the day laborer's is not: the day laborer must work in order to attain a basic level of functioning, while the heiress need not work in order to attain the same level of functioning. Even though the heiress does happen to spend her time engaged in paid work, the time she devotes to paid work is still available to her to pursue other ends if she so chooses. If, one day, she wishes to go to the beach instead of working, she possesses the free time to do so. Though the day laborer may also wish to go to the beach that day, she does not possess the free time to do so.

The heiress possesses the resource of free time despite spending much of her time engaged in paid work because she is free not to devote her time to work, and so she possesses the time to pursue other ends, while the day laborer does not possess the resource of free time because it is necessary for her to spend her time engaged in paid work, to the effect that she lacks the time to pursue any other ends.

Free time, so understood, is appropriately regarded as a resource because such time is generally required to pursue one's conception of the good, whatever it may be. Citizens require such time to pursue any ends beyond satisfying their basic needs. Someone who must spend all of one's time meeting one's basic needs generally lacks the time required for personal projects, relationships, moral, ethical, and political commitments, or any other pursuits.

At this point, one might object that free time is not necessary to pursue *every* conception of the good. One's conception of the good might involve spending all of one's time satisfying one's basic needs, and thus one would not need free time in order to pursue one's conception of the good.[6] To consider this objection, we can recognize three different relationships that might exist between the time one requires to satisfy one's basic needs and the time one requires to pursue one's conception of the good.

---

6 A similar objection has been raised against Rawls's description of income and wealth as all-purpose means necessary to pursue one's conception of the good: if one is a religious ascetic who disdains wealth, for instance, income and wealth are not necessary to pursue one's conception of the good. See Schwartz, "Moral Neutrality and Primary Goods," 294–307; Teitelman, "Limits of Individualism," 545–56; Freeman, *Rawls*, 152–54.

First, these two categories of time might be entirely distinct; one can pursue one's conception of the good only when one is not meeting one's basic needs. Say someone's conception of the good is solely to be a distinguished film expert, but that she cannot find a way to make a living watching and studying movies. The time she must spend to meet her basic needs does not overlap with the time she requires to pursue her conception of the good, so to pursue her conception of the good at all, she requires free time.

Second, these two categories might partially overlap; one can pursue some portion of one's conception of the good when one is also satisfying one's basic needs, but some portion one cannot. Say someone's conception of the good is to be a teacher, marathon runner, and dedicated friend. During some portion of the time he is teaching and running, he is also attaining the income and exercise to meet his financial and bodily basic needs. But during some portion of that time, he is pursuing only his conception of the good—say, his bodily need for exercise is satisfied by only part of the time he spends running. Moreover, as in the first case, he might be able to be a devoted friend only during time when he is not engaged in meeting his basic needs. In instances of complete disjoint and partial overlap, one does require free time to pursue one's conception of the good.

There may, however, third, be instances in which one can simultaneously satisfy one's basic needs while fully pursuing one's conception of the good. Say someone's conception of the good is to be a social worker and a parent, and that she spends all of her time meeting her and her children's basic needs, but in doing so she also fully pursues her conception of the good. In this case, she does not require free time to pursue her conception of the good, and thus, one can object that free time is not always required to pursue one's conception of the good.[7]

There are two possible responses to this objection, both of which are parallel to those commonly offered in response to the similar objection that has been raised against whether income and wealth are truly "all-purpose" resources, valuable whatever one's conception of the good. The first is to grant the point, but to contend that cases in which one's conception of the good entirely overlaps with satisfying one's basic needs are rare, and thus main-

---

7 One might take this objection further and contend that rather than being concerned that individuals have free time to pursue their conceptions of the good, we should instead try to align individuals' conceptions of the good with the time they must spend satisfying their basic needs, perhaps by making the necessary tasks of life—work, care, health—more satisfying and rewarding.

tain that free time is still *generally* required to pursue one's conception of the good.[8] This response effectively deflects the objection, for in order to qualify as a resource, the object in question must only be an input generally necessary to pursue one's conception of the good.

Though this response is sufficient, a further possible response is to again grant the point, but to argue that, even in these cases of complete overlap, free time is necessary to be able to *revise* one's conception of the good. To take the case of the social worker and parent, her conception of the good might change over time and she might come to want to spend more time with friends and on hobbies. Without free time, she does not have the ability to pursue a revised conception of the good. If instead she had free time, even if she spent it working and parenting, she would be able to pursue a revised conception of the good because she would have the free time available to reallocate to friends and hobbies. Thus, even if pursuing one's plan of life entirely overlaps with satisfying one's basic needs, to be genuinely able to revise one's conception of the good one requires free time. To state the same point somewhat differently, having free time serves to protect one's ability to revise one's conception of the good, thereby making one's ability to pursue one's plan of life more robust.[9]

Free time, understood as time not committed to meeting one's own or one's dependents' basic needs, is then prima facie appropriately recognized as a resource, for it is generally required to pursue one's conception of the good, whatever it may be.

3.3 RESOURCE CRITERIA

To the extent that the idea of time free from necessity has been developed in any detail—with more specificity than Marx's distinction between the "realm of freedom" and the "realm of necessity"[10]—it has primarily been

8 Rawls's description of primary goods takes this tack to avoid the objection: they are, he specifies, "generally necessary" to pursue one's conception of the good. See, for instance, *A Theory of Justice*, rev. ed. (Cambridge, MA: Belknap, 1999), 361.

9 Allen Buchanan, "Revisability and Rational Choice," *Canadian Journal of Philosophy* 5 (1975): 395–408. For the alternative idea of robustness, see Philip Pettit, *A Theory of Freedom and Government* (Oxford: Oxford University Press, 1997).

10 Karl Marx, *Capital*, vol. 3, in *Karl Marx: Selected Writings*, ed. David McLellan, 2nd ed. (Oxford: Oxford University Press, 2000), 535. See James C. Klagge, "Marx's Realms of 'Freedom' and 'Necessity,'" *Canadian Journal of Philosophy* 16 (1986): 769–77.

within the social scientific literatures, specifically among time-use researchers and sociologists. Drawing on these literatures, there are three ways that the idea of free time can be formulated: (1) as time not engaged in *typically necessary* activities, (2) as time not engaged in *subjectively necessary* activities, and (3) as time not engaged in *objectively necessary* activities.[11]

As noted at the outset of the chapter, there is no single correct conception of free time; instead, which conception is appropriate depends on the particular purposes to which it is applied. Thus, in order to arbitrate between the various formulations of free time, we must turn to the particular purposes to which the formulation is to be applied. That is, the aim is to identify a conception of free time *as a resource* to which individuals could plausibly have a claim as an object of a *public* and *feasible* theory of justice. To be such a resource, any good must satisfy three criteria: *the all-purpose criterion*, which requires that it is generally required to pursue any conception of the good, *the publicity criterion*, which requires that it is possible to reliably and verifiably know whether an individual possesses a given resource, and *the feasibility criterion*, which requires that it is possible to obtain such knowledge in a practical way. These constraints, which are drawn from Rawls's account of primary goods and are commonly applied in the distributive justice literature, provide a way to decide among the various formulations of free time.

The all-purpose criterion, following Section 2.2, does not require further elaboration, but the publicity and feasibility criteria must be specified further. First, consider another all-purpose resource that fails these two constraints: that is, any internal personal resource, like, for instance, self-respect or resilience. These internal personal qualities are indeed all-purpose resources: they are generally required to pursue any conception of the good. Yet such resources fail to meet the publicity and feasibility criteria. It is, first, not possible to reliably and verifiably know whether one possesses the given quality, and, second, even if it were possible, it is not possible to obtain this information in a practical way. Thus, even though something might properly be an

11 It is worth emphasizing that though these formulations are drawn from the time-use literature, the aim here is not to evaluate the social scientific constructions of free time as such, but to evaluate possible formulations for the purpose of developing an account of free time suitable to serve as a resource in a public and feasible theory of justice. As such, the constructions I consider depart from the social scientific formulations where appropriate for the purpose of the present analysis.

all-purpose resource, it may not be the type of resource one can have a claim to as an object of a public and feasible theory of justice.[12]

The publicity criterion (the epistemic constraint) requires that it is possible for an outside observer (i.e., the state) to reliably and verifiably know whether one possesses (and in what amount) a given resource. The reliability component ensures that it is possible to accurately know whether an individual possesses the resource, while the verifiability component ensures that it is possible to objectively know whether one possesses the resource. The feasibility criterion (the practicality constraint) requires that it is possible for an outside observer to obtain this knowledge in a practical way, meaning that it must be possible for an outside observer to noninvasively (without intrusions on privacy) and efficiently (without excessive effort) obtain this knowledge.[13]

In order to test the three contending formulations of free time, three sets of questions serve as guides:

First, to the all-purpose criterion, is it an input that is generally required to pursue any conception of the good? And, is the formulation accurately tailored to the quality that makes the resource all purpose? (This question tests whether the formulation meaningfully corresponds to the essential feature of a resource.)

Second, to the publicity criterion, when two individuals have the same time-affecting circumstances and in fact spend their time in precisely the same ways, does the formulation hold that the two individuals have the same amount of free time?[14] (This question tests whether the formulation allows for verifiable, i.e., objective, knowledge.) And, when two individuals have different time-affecting circumstances and in fact spend their time in

12 Thus, Rawls holds that citizens have a legitimate claim not to the resource of self-respect itself, but to the *social bases* of self-respect.

13 The publicity and feasibility constraints are both suggested by Rawls. The particular ways I have specified the two constraints follow elaborations on the Rawlsian constraints, specifically those by Arnold, "Difference Principle at Work," 94–118; Mathias Risse and Robert C. Hockett, "Primary Goods Revisited: The 'Political Problem' and Its Rawlsian Solution" (Cornell Law Faculty Publications, Paper 55, 2006); and Andrew Williams, "Incentives, Inequality, and Publicity," *Philosophy & Public Affairs* 27 (1998): 225–47. Risse and Hockett refer to both constraints combined as the "the publicity constraint," and Arnold refers to both again combined as "the workability test." G. A. Cohen describes the constraints as "the test of public checkability." Cohen, *Rescuing Justice and Equality*, 99n33.

14 Time-affecting circumstances are the factors that affect how much time it objectively takes one to meet one's basic needs. Such circumstances include, for instance, one's wage rate, whether one has a disability, and one's caregiving obligations. Excluded are one's values, tastes, and preferences. I discuss this further in 3.8.

different ways, does the formulation hold that the two individuals have different amounts of free time? (This question tests whether the formulation allows for reliable, i.e., accurate, knowledge.)

Third, to the feasibility criterion, is it possible for an outside observer to determine how much free time an individual has without entering a realm generally considered private and without spending a great amount of individually tailored time and effort to do so? (This question tests whether the formulation allows for a practical, i.e., noninvasive and efficient, assessment.)

3.4 TYPICALLY NECESSARY

The first formulation, employed by some time-use researchers, is the most straightforward. On this account, free time is all and only the time when one is not engaged in *typically necessary* activities. This formulation is in some sense a correction to the conception of leisure as all time not engaged in paid work, motivated by the recognition that other activities in addition to paid work are also generally necessary. The typically necessary activities can be divided into the categories of paid work, household and caregiving labor, and personal care, or following the terminology of time-use researchers, "contracted time," "committed time," and "necessary time." The first category encompasses all time engaged in paid work, including self-employment and commuting time; the second, housework, grocery shopping, cooking, and the like, as well as all caregiving; the third, sleep, eating, sex, exercise, and grooming.[15] The particular activities that qualify as typically necessary can be specified in a fine-grained fashion (with distinctions between, for instance, food preparation, meal cleanup, and cleaning house) or more broadly (for instance, all household work). Free time is the remainder after subtracting all time spent in paid work, household and caregiving labor, and personal care.[16]

However the particular categories are specified, the crucial feature of this formulation is that *all* time engaged in an activity categorized as typically necessary is deemed necessary, and thus not free time. If one, for instance, sleeps late, goes for long walks, takes lengthy naps and baths, and devotes

15 Dagfinn Ås, "Studies of Time-Use: Problems and Prospects," *Acta Sociologica* 21 (1978): 125–41.

16 For an example of this measure of free time in time-use studies, see John P. Robinson and Geoffrey Godbey, *Time for Life: The Surprising Ways Americans Use Their Time*, 2nd ed. (University Park: Pennsylvania State University Press, 1999), 123–26, 355–63.

hours to preparing and slowly savoring elaborate three-course meals, so long as each of these activities is categorized as one of the typically necessary activities (i.e., sleeping, exercising, grooming, cooking, eating), all of the time one engages in these activities qualifies as necessary. Because each activity is typically necessary, none of the time engaged in these activities qualifies as free time.

Though this formulation of free time does meet the publicity criterion, as it would be possible to reliably and verifiably know how much time individuals spend in the typically necessary activities, and possibly the feasibility criterion, if this knowledge could be obtained noninvasively and efficiently, more important, it fails to meet the all-purpose criterion. Time not engaged in typically necessary activities is not an input that is generally required to pursue any conception of the good, and so is not appropriately understood as a resource.

Many different plans of life are compatible with lacking any time not engaged in typically necessary activities: from the life of the pleasure seeker (with all one's time engaged in sleeping, eating, exercising, grooming, and so forth) to the life of the consummate worker (with nearly all one's time engaged in working and commuting, and a small amount devoted to sleeping, eating, and grooming) and the life of the moderate (with all one's time devoted to working, caregiving, exercising, cleaning, cooking, eating, grooming, and sleeping, all in balanced proportions).

Even if it were possible to refine the categories such that the pursuit of most conceptions of the good did require time not engaged in typically necessary activities, this conception is not appropriately tailored to the quality that makes the resource of free time all-purpose: that the time is not consumed by necessity. Much of the time that individuals spend engaged in typically necessary activities is neither experienced as necessary nor, one might be inclined to say, "actually" necessary. Though some portion of the time one spends sleeping or eating, for instance, is objectively necessary to live and is experienced as such, often some other portion is neither experienced as necessary nor objectively necessary—think of dozing in a hammock on a Sunday afternoon or eating a dessert one can barely finish after a full meal. Such periods of sleeping or eating, though spent in typically necessary activities, are more appropriately regarded as a use of one's free time.

Because it cannot provide a way to meaningfully distinguish between necessary and unnecessary activities, the formulation of free time as time not engaged in typically necessary activities is, like its relative, time not engaged in paid work, more appropriately described as a specific good.[17] Indeed, since all that remains after one subtracts typically necessary activities from one's time are conventional recreational activities, this formulation is not appropriate as a way to specify the conception of free time as a resource.

3.5 SUBJECTIVELY NECESSARY

The second formulation corresponds to the idea that one might experience the time engaged in some activities as necessary; that is, it specifies free time as the time not engaged in *subjectively necessary* activities.[18] This formulation tracks the recent research in sociology (as well as the common complaints) that individuals in modern society commonly experience a "time bind," "time pressure," or a "time crunch," feeling as though they never have enough time to do everything that must be done or any time to do the things that they want to do.[19] The idea is that if someone believes there is something she must do and experiences the time doing it as entirely constrained by necessity—even if it is not objectively necessary—that time is not free.

Thus stated, the formulation of free time as the time not engaged in subjectively necessary activities can be specified further depending on what one judges the activities in question to be necessary *for*. As a first take, the formulation could be specified so that free time is any time not engaged in activities that one judges or experiences as necessary to pursue *any value or aim*

17 The same arguments hold against treating time not engaged in paid work as a resource. Even if one attempted to recast time not engaged in paid work as a resource, on the thought that such time is generally required to pursue one's conception of the good, it would be inappropriate to recognize such time as a resource because it is not tailored to the feature that would ostensibly make it all-purpose (that it is time not constrained by necessity).

18 Note that the generic description of this formulation ("subjectively necessary") conflates time that one *experiences as* necessary with time that one *judges to be* necessary. These variations may pry apart: one could, conceivably, experience time as necessary without actually judging it to be necessary, just as one could, perhaps more plausibly, judge time to be necessary, but not experience it as such. Given, however, that typically one only experiences time as necessary that one judges to be necessary (and vice versa), and given that this distinction does not bear on the discussion that follows, I treat each variation as part of a single formulation: free time as time that is not engaged in subjectively necessary activities.

19 See, for instance, Arlie Russell Hochschild, *The Time Bind: When Work Becomes Home and Home Becomes Work* (New York: Metropolitan Books, 1997) and Robinson and Godbey, *Time for Life*, 229–86.

that one happens to hold. But this specification is obviously too broad. Imagine someone who values being current on the latest novels and so thinks that it is necessary to spend three hours a day reading these novels. Even if she sometimes did not want to spend time reading and viewed the activity as a chore, we should be loath to describe such time as constrained by necessity even in the subjective sense at issue.

In response, the formulation could be revised so that free time is any time not engaged in activities that one experiences as necessary to pursue one's *comprehensive* values or aims.[20] Yet again, the specification is too broad. Consider, for instance, a long-time regular marathon runner who chooses where to live and what career to pursue based on how frequently it would allow her to run. The value of being a marathon runner is a comprehensive one as it plays a large part in her life. Nonetheless, again, the time she spends training does not correspond to the idea of subjectively necessary time in the relevant sense.

Instead, the appropriate way of specifying the subjective formulation is that free time is the time when one is not engaged in activities that one judges to be and experiences as necessary to meet what one judges to be the necessities of life. This formulation of free time is subjective in two ways: what counts as free time is relative to the individual's own judgment about what the necessities of life are and to the individual's own judgment about and experience of the tasks that are necessary to achieve those ends.[21] Say one thinks that having a spotless house is a necessity of life and judges three hours cleaning per day to be necessary to attain such a level of household cleanliness. Because he judges and experiences the time he spends cleaning as necessary, on this formulation all of the time he spends cleaning qualifies as necessary time, and thus as not free time.

This formulation of free time may meet the all-purpose criterion—it is possible that one generally requires time that one does not experience as constrained by necessity to pursue one's conception of the good—but it fails the

---

20 Raz, *Morality of Freedom*, 288–320; see also the discussion in T. M. Scanlon, *What We Owe to Each Other* (Cambridge, MA: Belknap, 2000), 118–24.

21 This formulation could be altered to be subjective on only one of these prongs. That is, free time could be the time when one is not engaged in activities that one judges to be necessary to meet one's objective basic needs, or free time could be the time when one is not engaged in activities that are objectively necessary to meet what one judges to be the necessaries of life. Since the evaluation of the subjective formulation does not depend on which version one uses, I refer to the maximally subjective formulation.

publicity and feasibility criteria. The answers to each of the test questions for these criteria are negative.

First, to publicity, because how much free time one has depends, on this formulation, on an individual's own experiences and judgments, when considering either two individuals with the same or different time-affective circumstances and actual time usages, an outside observer could not determine whether the individuals have the same or different amounts of free time.

Consider, for instance, A and B, best friends who live in the same apartment building and rent identical units. Neither has children or a partner, both work the same number of hours for the same pay, and neither has a disability. A and B do everything together, including exercising together for two hours a day. A and B have the same time-affecting circumstances and spend their time in identical ways, but the subjective formulation may not hold that they have the same amounts of free time. Say A judges all of their time exercising to be necessary to attain the basic need of physical fitness and experiences it as such, while B thinks only half of it is necessary and experiences the latter half as not necessary and only done for fun. According to the subjective formulation, A and B have different amounts of free time even though they have the same time-affecting circumstances and spend their time in exactly the same way.

Alternately, take the same case but now say that A has a disability (she is blind) while B does not, and that A now devotes one hour a day to learning how to use a service dog while B spends that time relaxing. They now have different time-affecting circumstances and different time usages, but again the formulation does not necessarily hold that they actually have different amounts of free time. If, say, A does not judge or experience her training with the service dog as necessary to attain the basic need of physical mobility (she just thinks of it as a fun thing to do), her time spent training qualifies as free time in the same way as B's time relaxing.

Second, to feasibility, in either version of the example, an outside observer could not noninvasively or efficiently determine how much free time either A or B has. Even if it were technically possible to obtain the relevant knowledge, to do so would require entering a realm generally considered private (their personal thoughts and experiences) and would require a great amount of individually-tailored time and effort (individually and continuously monitoring their thoughts and experiences). The subjective formulation—free time as time not engaged in subjectively necessary activities—thus fails both the publicity and the feasibility criteria. As such, even if it were an all-purpose input, it is not appropriately recognized as a resource to which citizens could plausibly have claims on a public and feasible theory of justice.

3.6 OBJECTIVELY NECESSARY

The third way to develop the idea of free time is as the time that is not committed to activities that are *objectively necessary* to attain the necessities of life. Here the idea is that, for any individual, there is some amount of time that must be devoted to necessary activities in order to meet a basic level of functioning in one's society. In contrast with the subjective formulations, this approach is objective in that the amount of time it is necessary to spend to meet the threshold level of functioning is determined without reference to an individual's own judgment or experience of how much time is necessary. It is instead objectively determined, and there are two ways such an objective determination can be made: the social benchmark approach and the basic needs approach. On both approaches, the operative sense of "necessary" is not a physical or logical one, but a social one: it is necessary to spend some amount of time on the necessary activities in order to function and participate in one's society.

The first way of determining how much time it is objectively necessary to spend on the necessary activities, the social benchmark approach, was recently developed by Robert E. Goodin, James Mahmud Rice, Antti Parpo, and Lina Eriksson as a way for time-use researchers to measure "discretionary time."[22] On this approach, there are three categories of necessary activities—paid labor, unpaid household labor, and personal care—and there is some amount of time it is necessary for one to spend engaged in each. One's free time (or discretionary time) is "the amount of time you have left over, once you have done what is strictly necessary in each of those three realms."[23] Essential to the social benchmark approach, how much time it is necessary to spend in each of these necessary activities is determined solely with reference to the amount of time people in one's society actually spend doing these activities.

22 Goodin et al., *Discretionary Time*; see also Robert E. Goodin, James Mahmud Rice, Michael Bittman, and Peter Saunders, "The Time-Pressure Illusion: Discretionary Time vs. Free Time," *Social Indicators Research* 73 (2005): 43–70.

23 Goodin et al., *Discretionary Time*, 35, and 34–53. Goodin et al. do not use "discretionary time" interchangeably with "free time," as I do here; they instead use "free time" to refer to what they and I both label "spare time" (see 3.7).

The approach follows the method to determine a relative poverty line (that is, a poverty threshold set with reference only to the median income, and not any absolute measure of deprivation). Indeed, the approach uses the poverty line directly for the first category, paid labor: the necessary amount of time to spend engaged in paid labor is the amount of time it is necessary to work to earn a poverty level income, indexed to one's wage rate. For the second category, unpaid household labor, this approach uses the poverty line as a model: the necessary amount of time to spend engaged in household labor is 50 percent of the median amount of time individuals in a society spend in these tasks, indexed to household structure. If, for example, the median amount of time single individuals without children actually spent on household activities was twenty hours per week, the necessary amount of time for any individual with that household structure to spend on household activities would be ten hours per week. For the third category, personal care, because the amount of time people spend on these tasks is more inelastic, the necessary amount of time to spend engaged in personal care is set at 80 percent of the median amount of time individuals in a society spend in these tasks.

More important than the specifics of the method Goodin et al. propose are two general features of the social benchmark approach. First, how much time it is objectively necessary for one to spend in the necessary activities is set entirely relative to how people in one's society spend their time. Thus, if the median amount of time people in one society spend on personal care is 84 hours per week and in another society it is 56 hours per week, the amount of time it is objectively necessary for an individual to spend on personal care can be known based solely on these facts and the amount is different between the two societies (67.2 hours and 44.8 hours, respectively). Second, following from this, one can determine how much time it is objectively necessary for an individual to spend in the three necessary activities without any knowledge of the particulars of the individual's situation, aside from her wage rate and household structure.

The second formulation, the basic needs approach, rather than relying on how much time people in a society in fact spend engaged in the necessary activities, instead begins with certain objective basic needs, which are the demands that generally must be met to function at a basic or minimally decent level in one's society. Meeting the basic needs requires time, either directly, as with sleep and exercise, or indirectly, as with material goods purchased with labor earnings. For each individual, meeting one's basic needs objectively requires a certain amount of time. Free time is the time beyond what it is objectively necessary for one to spend to meet one's (or one's dependents') basic needs.

How much time it is objectively necessary to spend engaged in various tasks to attain the basic needs depends on the particulars of an individual's circumstances. It may, for instance, take someone with a disability more time to meet his household and bodily basic needs, someone with a small apartment less time to meet her household basic needs, someone with a long commute more time to meet his financial basic needs, and so forth. On this approach, there is a certain amount of time that it is objectively necessary to spend in various activities to attain the basic needs, and this amount of time will vary between individuals based on their circumstances. (I discuss which circumstances are relevant to this assessment in 3.8.)

The determination of how much time it is objectively necessary for individuals in particular circumstances to spend to meet the basic needs is not, unlike on the social benchmark approach, determined purely relatively. For any of the basic needs, but for household and bodily necessary activities in particular, relative dimensions may be taken into account, as how much time individuals in given circumstances spend on average in necessary activities does provide meaningful guidance as to what is socially necessary to function in one's society. But, importantly, the determination of how much time is objectively necessary could also be informed by other considerations, namely democratic or expert judgment. Say, for instance, the median amount of time full-time employed parents spend on grocery shopping, cooking, and eating is only five hours per week. The assessment of how much time is objectively necessary might reflect that, but also could be adjusted by democratic or expert judgment about how much time it is necessary to spend preparing and eating food for adequate nutrition. Similar adjustments could be made in cases in which individuals generally might, due to competitive pressures or other social norms, spend either more time or less time than is objectively necessary to meet a basic need. A purely relative determination of objective necessity is potentially responsive to spurious social factors, and the basic needs approach allows for other considerations to be taken into account to correct for this.

The social benchmark approach does not fully satisfy each of the resource criteria, while the basic needs approach, if it is not excessively individually tailored, does meet all of the criteria. The social benchmark approach satisfies the feasibility criterion, but only partially satisfies the publicity criterion, failing the reliability component. The basic needs approach satisfies the publicity criterion, and while it does pose potential difficulties for the feasibility criterion, can meet it if appropriately implemented.

The social benchmark approach does meet the publicity criterion's verifiability test, for when two individuals face the same time-affecting circumstances and have the same time usages, this approach does hold that they have the same amount of free time. It also meets the feasibility test, as it is possible for an outside observer to determine how much free time one has in a noninvasive and efficient manner. One must first determine the median amount of time individuals in different household structures and at different wage rates spend in each of the necessary activities (which could be learned through time-use surveys), and then for any individual, only her household structure and wage rate.

The social benchmark approach does not, however, satisfy the reliability component, which requires that it is possible to accurately know how much free time one has. When two individuals face different time-affecting circumstances and different actual time usages, this formulation does not necessarily hold that they have different amounts of free time. When A and B face different circumstances and accordingly spend their time in different ways (when, for instance, A is disabled), this formulation still holds that they have the same amounts of free time, even though A spends an hour per day training the service dog while B relaxes. The social benchmark approach is sensitive only to variations across wage rates and household structures, so it cannot be responsive to the difference in A and B's circumstances as a result of A's disability. Even if the social benchmark approach were revised to attend to more fine-grained variations in circumstances, it would still track only the median amount of time people in those circumstances spend on the necessary activities, and thus may not reliably correspond to how much time individuals in particular circumstances must actually spend to meet the necessities of life. Accordingly, this approach cannot reliably—that is, accurately—track how much free time individuals possess.

The basic needs approach, by contrast, meets both the reliability and verifiability components of the publicity criterion. This approach holds that A and B have the same amounts of free time when they face the same time-affecting circumstances and spend their time identically, and when A and B do not face the same time-affecting circumstances and do not spend their time in the same ways (when A is disabled), it holds that they have different amounts of free time. Because physical mobility is a basic need, and so long as training with a service dog is recognized as objectively necessary for A to attain physical mobility, the time A spends training is objectively necessary to meet a basic need, and thus not free time.

Whether the basic needs approach meets the feasibility criterion depends on how it is formulated. If it is maximally sensitive to variations in individuals' circumstances, it may not be possible for an outside observer to determine how much free time one has in a noninvasive and efficient manner. To take the example of A's time training with the service dog, if A were unusually inept at learning how to work with the service dog, the amount of time it is objectively necessary for her to spend training is longer than the amount of time for someone who is unusually adept. An outside observer, that is, the state, would then have to know A's aptitude for training the dog to determine how much time it is objectively necessary for her to spend to meet her basic needs. This case may not be particularly problematic, if, say, it is not unacceptably invasive for the state to rely on a teacher's assessment, but consider the invasiveness and effort of determining how much time a given individual must spend to attain, for instance, the basic needs of personal hygiene, household cleanliness, or nutrition. If maximally individually tailored, the basic needs approach runs aground on the feasibility criterion.

If the basic needs approach is instead moderately tailored to relevant individual circumstances, it is possible to meet the feasibility criterion. That is, rather than relying on how much time is objectively necessary for given individual A to meet her basic need of physical mobility, to be feasible, the approach should rely on how much time is objectively necessary for individuals in a set of relevant circumstances (e.g., blind people learning to use a service dog) to meet the basic need of physical mobility. (Though only moderately individually tailored, as long as the assessment is tailored to the relevant circumstances—as I discuss in 3.8—the approach still meets the reliability component.) In this way, the basic needs approach requires only determining how much time is necessary for individuals in given circumstances to meet their basic needs and then what circumstances obtain for any given individual, information that can noninvasively and efficiently be obtained, meeting the feasibility criterion.

The basic needs approach, when moderately individually tailored, does accordingly meet each of the components of the publicity and feasibility criteria, surpassing the other approaches. As a new conception of free time, it now requires further elaboration—the task of the next section.

3.7 THE DEFINITION OF FREE TIME

Free time is the time beyond that which it is objectively necessary for one to spend to meet one's own basic needs, or the basic needs of one's dependents, whether with necessary paid work, household labor, or personal care. I refer to free time more concisely as the time not committed to meeting one's own, or one's dependents', basic needs. The inverse of free time is necessary time. The assessment of how much free time one has is determined by how much time it is objectively necessary for one to spend, taking account of relevant circumstances, to meet one's own, and one's dependents', basic needs.

Basic needs are the material needs one must meet in order to attain a basic level of functioning in one's society. The needs and the level of functioning are, as such, both biologically and socially determined. The basic needs are the same for all adults within a given society, but can vary between societies in accordance with local circumstances and norms. The basic needs can, for ease of reference, be divided into three categories: bodily needs, household needs, and financial needs. There are corresponding necessary activities to meet each basic need: sleeping, exercising, eating, grooming, and so on; cooking, cleaning, maintenance, and so on; and paid work and financial management, and so forth. These categories serve only as a heuristic. They are fluid, as one can potentially satisfy one's basic needs in one domain through activity in another domain, and one need not spend time engaged in activities in each domain. To state this more formally, using the case of a wage-earner, $FTi_h = 24$ hours $- (Ni_h + C_\$/Wi_{\$/h})$, where FTi is how much free time individual i has in a day, Ni is how much time i must spend to satisfy the basic needs i satisfies directly, C is the cost of the goods or services i must purchase to satisfy i's other basic needs, and Wi is i's wage rate. How much free time one has is determined by how much time one must spend to meet one's basic needs, not how much time one actually spends meeting one's basic needs.[24]

---

24 This is important to note for two reasons. First, say someone adapts to having no free time by spending less time than is objectively necessary to meet her basic needs, thereby barely meeting or failing to meet her basic needs (e.g., by sleeping little and giving up on household tasks). If free time were determined with reference to actual time usage, she would thereby be regarded as gaining free time, allowing for the perverse implication that one could obtain one's fair share of free time by failing to meet one's basic needs. Second, relying on actual time

How much free time one has increases as the amount of time it is necessary for one to spend meeting one's basic needs decreases. As such, social arrangements could alter how much free time individuals have either by directly providing for a basic need (e.g., direct provision of housing or caregiving) or by making a basic need more efficiently obtainable (e.g., higher wages or a faster transportation system). At the limit, if it were not necessary for one to spend any time engaged in necessary activities in order to meet one's basic needs, one would have complete free time (though this is, at least as yet, physiologically impossible).

Free time is not the same thing as spare time. Free time is the time not committed to objectively necessary activities to meet one's basic needs—to *necessary* paid work, household labor, or personal care. Spare time is the time when one is not engaged in any typically necessary activity—in *any* paid work, household labor, or personal care. Free time is to be distinguished from spare time because the above-necessary amount of time spent in typically necessary activities is discretionary, and so properly understood as a use of one's free time. If one spends more time engaged in the typically necessary activities than is objectively necessary to meet one's basic needs—as is often the case—one would have less spare time than free time. For instance, if one, to return to the example in 3.4, sleeps, exercises, cooks, and eats for more time than is objectively necessary to meet one's bodily basic needs, one would have more free time than spare time. By contrast, if one spends less time engaged in the typically necessary activities than is objectively necessary to meet one's basic needs, one would have more spare time than free time. For instance, say one, discouraged by persistent time scarcity, gives up on trying to meet one's household and bodily basic needs, and spends less time than is objectively necessary sleeping, eating, and cleaning. In this case, one would have less free time than spare time.[25]

Some portion of the time one spends engaged in an activity may—and often will—qualify as necessary time and some as free time. If, for example, the basic need of health requires, for one without exceptional bodily needs,

---

usage would run afoul of the feasibility criterion, since it would be invasive and costly to obtain knowledge of how much time individuals actually spend on necessary activities.

25 An implication is that if someone is unemployed and does not have another adequate income source, or receives unemployment benefits only on the condition of searching for and accepting available work, it is still, in the relevant sense, objectively necessary for her to work to obtain an adequate income. The time she does not spend working or searching for work is additional spare time, but it is not free time.

eight hours of sleep and thirty minutes of exercise per day, if one sleeps and exercises for an additional three hours per day, that time is a use of one's free time. This applies to any necessary activity, though an important qualification applies to paid work. Say someone earns twenty dollars per hour and must earn four hundred dollars per week to meet her basic needs, and her employer gives her the choice of working between twenty and forty hours per week. If she chooses to work forty hours per week, twenty of those hours quality as necessary time and twenty as free time. If, however, her employer required her to work forty hours per week, even though she would earn an above-necessary income, all forty of her work hours would qualify as necessary time. By requiring her to work longer hours, her employer effectively makes the longer hours what is objectively necessary to meet her basic needs. (I return to this important point in 4.4.)

As such, to divide the time one spends engaged in an activity between necessary and free time, it must be the case that one can freely choose to spend only the properly necessary amount of time engaged in the activity. If one cannot, the effectively necessary time is whatever amount of time one can choose to engage in the necessary activity to meet the basic need. In these instances, the time one is engaged in such effectively necessary activities is not free time. Thus, an additional way social arrangements can increase how much free time one has is by making it the case that one can in fact choose to spend no more time than is objectively necessary engaged in a necessary activity.

3.8 TAKING ACCOUNT OF RESPONSIBILITY

The basic needs approach requires that the assessment of how much time it is objectively necessary to spend to meet one's basic needs is moderately tailored to relevant individual circumstances. This raises the question of which circumstances are relevant to that assessment. To see the significance of this question, consider how the approach could be responsive, or not, to whether one has a disability, to the grooming standards of one's social position, to the maintenance requirements of one's particular home, to one's occupation and the range of one's occupational choices, to one's level of wealth, and to whether and how one came to have dependents, among other factors. For any individual, some circumstances may reflect unavoidable realities, while others are, to varying degrees, the results of one's own choices. Assessing how much free time individuals have—not only on the basic needs approach, but any reliable formulation—thus unavoidably raises the question of how sensitive the approach ought to be to individual responsibility.

Liberal egalitarian theories of justice take different positions on the extent to which citizens' claims to resources ought to be sensitive to their choices. As such, the definition of free time itself ought not and does not favor or preclude particular positions about responsibility-sensitivity. But given the unavoidability and significance of this question, it is important to sketch how a formulation of free time might—and how I will—address these issues of individual responsibility. Broadly, the range of possible time-affecting circumstances can be divided into three categories: first, those that any approach ought to be sensitive to; second, those that an approach, given additional argument, ought to be responsive to; and third, those that an approach might defer judgment on to democratic decision in light of empirical conditions.

In the first category are those circumstances that, consistent with the more responsibility-sensitive positions, would generally be taken to be unchosen from the individual's perspective. A nonexhaustive list of such circumstances includes how much time one must engage in paid work to meet one's financial basic needs, given one's personal wealth, abilities, and the existing labor market. It is relevant, for instance, if one has no personal wealth and must work to meet one's basic needs, if one can command only a low wage and so must work long hours, or if one can only find employment that otherwise requires long hours. Also included among these circumstances is how time-intensive, as a result of material constraints, it is to meet one's household needs, such as if one cannot afford time-saving appliances (e.g., in-home laundry machine and dishwasher) or conveniences (e.g., prepared foods, home maintenance and repair services), or if one can afford to live only where the demands of home maintenance are more onerous (e.g., somewhere rural or run-down), or, related to this, if one can afford to live only somewhere with a long commute to one's workplace. And these circumstances include whether one has a disability or illness that affects how time-consuming it is to meet one's basic needs, as with a mobility impairment that makes it take longer to do many everyday tasks or with an illness that requires spending additional time on medical care or treatment.[26]

---

26 If a theory were *maximally* responsibility sensitive, each of these circumstances could be refined to specify that they must be in no way a result of one's own choices.

The first category also, I argue, includes whether one has primary responsibility as a caregiver for dependents, excluding one's own procreative children (whose care, as I will discuss, falls into the second category). Some people, specifically the ill, disabled, and elderly infirm, are not able to, or cannot reasonably be expected to, meet their basic needs themselves. Other people must provide for or help them to meet their basic needs. On any liberal egalitarian theory of justice, and as I here assume, society has a general obligation to ensure, insofar as doing so is consistent with the other requirements of justice, that the basic needs are met of those who are not able to meet those needs themselves. This general obligation entails that, in addition to the set of necessary activities one must do to meet one's own basic needs, there is another set of necessary activities that must be done to meet the basic needs of those who are not able to.

Some people take on this general social obligation and provide unpaid caregiving to their own close relations—their spouses, their parents, their relatives, during periods of illness or elderly infirmity (continuing to set aside child care for the moment). Even if one may be regarded as taking on this responsibility voluntarily, such unpaid basic caregiving, that is, that which meets basic needs, is part of a social obligation. It is, as such, appropriately recognized as a necessary activity—a subtraction from one's own free time—because it is indeed an activity that is objectively necessary to meet basic needs, only the basic needs of someone else rather than oneself.[27] Because society has a general obligation to meet these basic needs, consistent with standard liberal egalitarian principles, any account of free time ought to be responsive to whether one is a primary caregiver for any dependents (again, still excluding procreative children). The definition of free time thus includes that free time is the time not committed to meeting one's own, or one's dependents', basic needs. To make the treatment of such unpaid basic caregiving as necessary time consistent with the publicity and feasibility criteria for free time as a resource, necessary caregiving could be limited to those who are legally recognized as one's dependents in this sense.[28]

27 See Stuart White's argument for treating caregiving as necessary civic labor. White, *The Civic Minimum: On the Rights and Obligations of Economic Citizenship* (Oxford: Oxford University Press, 2003), 109–12.

28 One's legal dependents should not, then, be understood narrowly as those who depend on one's income. A just society may have various regulations concerning legal dependency, limiting either the number or type of dependency relationships one can have, to either discourage or encourage private unpaid caregiving. For an argument for facilitating voluntary

As for procreative children, some responsibility-sensitive theories hold that the social obligation to meet the basic needs of those who are not able to applies differently to children than it does to adults. That is because particular citizens, namely the parents, are responsible for creating that obligation. As such, it is argued, they ought to be held responsible for the costs of that choice, and should be required to use their own resources to meet the basic needs of their children. It would be inappropriate, on this view, to treat caregiving for one's procreative children as a necessary activity, because the parents are not voluntarily discharging a social obligation—instead, they voluntarily created a new obligation. As such, the first category, those circumstances that any approach ought to be sensitive to, includes only responsibility for nonprocreative dependents.[29]

Any account of free time ought to be responsive to these individual circumstances in the first category, while it is possible for an account to treat any circumstances beyond this minimum as irrelevant. As such, so that the argument applies regardless of one's position on responsibility, when developing the book's core argument—that citizens are entitled to a fair share of free time—in the following chapter, I refer only to how one's free time is affected by these minimal circumstances. There are, however, other circumstances that an approach could treat as relevant to assessing how much free time one has, and these additional circumstances can be divided into the two remaining categories: those to which an approach, given additional argument, ought to be responsive, and those on which an approach might defer judgment. Different approaches might treat different circumstances as relevant and divide them into these two categories differently.

I will argue, after establishing the core argument, that two additional circumstances ought to be treated as relevant to a theory's assessment of how much free time individuals have: the terms of employment within one's chosen occupation and whether one has dependent procreative children.

---

at-home caregiving for the ill and infirm, see Norman Daniels, "Family Responsibility Initiatives and Justice Between Age Groups," *Law, Medicine and Health Care* 153 (1985): 153–59.

29 This discussion of children raises the question of whether children themselves have claims to free time. I will focus on the claims of adult citizens and will not take a position on this question, but one might hold that children, like adults, have claims to free time to pursue their age-specific conceptions of the good (as with play) and to determine their ultimate conceptions of the good (with explorative and mimicking play and unstructured time). Alternately, one might hold that children are not entitled to free time as such, but rather to having their developmental basic needs met, and that such play and unstructured time are among these basic needs.

To preview, first, I will argue in 4.7 that if one chooses to work in an occupation that pays less or requires longer hours than another one could have chosen, the assessment of how much free time one has ought to reflect the occupation one has in fact chosen, not that which one could have chosen. If one chooses to be a low-paid gardener, for instance, when one is, or could have been, qualified to be a high-paid doctor, one's free time ought to be determined with respect to the available terms of employment for gardeners, not doctors. Second, as I will argue in 6.4, procreative children ought to be treated as other dependents, with their basic care treated not as a use of one's free time, but as necessary time.

Beyond these, I argue that other circumstances ought to be deferred to democratic decision within particular empirical conditions. Personal wealth is one such circumstance: a society might democratically decide that if one has personal wealth above some amount, any paid work one does ought to be treated as a use of one's free time, rather than as necessary time. The threshold amount of wealth might be set higher or lower, or include or exclude different assets, depending on the society's resources and values. Many other circumstances, especially when assessed at the final level of policy specificity, might be treated this way. To take housing as an example, a society might hold that time spent maintaining a household up to a certain size and condition ought to qualify as necessary time, and any time spent maintaining multiple, larger, or more luxurious households ought to be treated as a use of one's free time. However, if a society had a deteriorating housing stock and determined that it would be socially valuable for people to devote time to improving the existing housing supply, the additional time spent repairing and renovating old buildings could be treated as necessary time.

Finally, the assessment of how much free time one has is generally not affected by one's level of efficiency or personal standards, unless these factors are regarded as or affected by a relevant circumstance (e.g., disability). To take an example, if two individuals have the same household cleaning demands and means of meeting them, but one is unusually efficient and the other unusually inefficient, their different efficiency levels would not affect the assessment of how much free time they have. Similarly, if two individuals again have the same household cleaning demands and means, but one has unusually high personal standards for cleanliness and one has unusually low standards, that too would not affect how much free time they have. An inefficient person or one with high standards is treated as spending some of her free time cleaning, and so has less free time than spare time, while an efficient person or one with low standards spends less time cleaning than is regarded as necessary, and so has more spare time than free time.

3.9 CONCLUSION

When free time is recognized as an all-purpose resource to which citizens could plausibly have claims in a public and feasible theory of justice, significant implications follow. Liberal egalitarian theories of justice can no longer ignore free time, relegating it to the domain of specific goods that individuals might choose or not in accordance with their particular understandings of the good life. The resource of free time has, instead, at least a presumptive claim to be, as Walzer offered, "a central issue of distributive justice." I turn now to vindicating that claim.

CHAPTER 4

THE CLAIM TO FREE TIME

4.1 MATERIAL AND TEMPORAL RESOURCES

Just as citizens generally require income and wealth to take advantage of their formal liberties and opportunities, so too do citizens generally require free time. In order to go to the polls, the meetinghouse, or the church; to run for political office or campaign for a cause; to associate with others in private spaces; to obtain educational and career qualifications; indeed, to do any of the things one is legally permitted to do, one generally requires some amount of both material resources and free time. Empirical political science has taken appropriate notice of this simple observation, including citizens' access to the resources of both money and time in standard models of political participation.[1] Yet, normative political philosophy, while extensively considering citizens' requirements for income and wealth, has scarcely noted citizens' corresponding requirements for time.

This silence is particularly surprising among liberal theorists of distributive justice, for ever since early socialist critics of liberalism levied the charge that the canon of liberal rights guaranteed nothing but "empty" freedoms, they have advanced distributive principles to guarantee all citizens access to the resources necessary to exercise their liberties. Nearly all theories of distributive justice endorse, what we may call, the *effective freedoms principle*: citizens have legitimate claims to a fair share of the resources generally re-

1 Sidney Verba, Kay Lehman Schlozman, and Henry E. Brady, *Voice and Equality: Civic Voluntarism in American Politics* (Cambridge, MA: Harvard University Press, 1995).

quired to exercise their formal liberties and opportunities. Characteristic of this fundamental principle's wide support, John Rawls contends that *any* reasonable theory of justice must provide "measures ensuring for all citizens adequate all-purpose means to make effective use of their freedoms."[2]

In satisfying the effective freedoms principle, however, theories of distributive justice have focused almost exclusively on the material resources citizens require, frequently equating "all-purpose means" with only the narrower resources of income and wealth, without any attention to the resource of time. Even theories that do not take such an exclusive focus on income and wealth, and that broaden the scope of requisite means to include a wider range of social conditions, still tend to make, at most, passing and oblique references to citizens' requirements for temporal resources.

The aim of this chapter is to argue that this neglect of time is a mistake. Free time is an all-purpose means in precisely the same way as income and wealth. It is, as I argued in 3.2, a resource that is generally required for the pursuit of one's chosen ends, whatever those may be. Free time is, more specifically, a resource that is generally required to exercise one's formal liberties and opportunities. As such, if one endorses the effective freedoms principle, as almost all theorists of distributive justice do, then one ought to hold that all citizens have legitimate claims to free time.

The argument is, however, not limited to this claim, for distributive theorists' inattention to time is not a mere case of neglect. Instead, theorists of distributive justice have given little attention to time because they have implicitly assumed what we may call the *time-money substitutability claim*: realizing a just distribution of income and wealth is sufficient to ensure a just distribution of free time. If the time-money substitutability claim were true, there would be nothing objectionable in a theory of justice attending only to the distribution of income and wealth without giving any distinct attention to free time.

It may be obscure how realizing a just distribution of one resource could also ensure a just distribution of a different resource, but the claim's plausibility is readily apparent if one considers the commonplace axiom "time is money."[3] Theories of distributive justice have taken this as a truism, treating

---

2 John Rawls, "The Idea of Public Reason Revisited," in Rawls, *Law of Peoples* (Cambridge, MA: Harvard University Press, 1999), 141.

3 The maxim "time is money" is commonly attributed to Benjamin Franklin's 1748 "Advice to a Young Tradesman, Written by an Old One," though the earliest known statement is from a 1719 issue of the periodical *Free-Thinker*. Franklin reproduced the passage from the

time and money as fungible goods, to the effect that one can use money to "purchase" time, either indirectly by forgoing income-earning work or directly by consuming time-saving goods and services. The time-money substitutability claim depends on this economic view of time, for the claim would be true if two corresponding claims about the functioning of economic markets were true. First, the *perfect divisibility of labor demand*: all individuals can freely choose to reduce their hours of paid work to the level they prefer. Second, the *perfect substitutability of money and basic needs satisfaction:* all individuals can unobjectionably meet their household and bodily basic needs by purchasing goods or services in the marketplace. If these two claims were true, so too would be the time-money substitutability claim, and theories of distributive justice would not be in error in attending to only the distribution of income and wealth.

I argue, however, that neither of these crucial assumptions about economic markets can be sustained, and that, as a result, theories of distributive justice cannot assume the time-money substitutability claim. Realizing a just distribution of income and wealth is insufficient to ensure a just distribution of free time. As such, theories of distributive justice cannot attend to only the distribution of income and wealth without any concern for the distribution of free time. Instead, to ensure that all citizens have the free time the exercise of their formal liberties requires—in order to guarantee that all citizens possess *both* the material and temporal "means to make effective use of their freedoms"—theories of justice must treat free time as a *distinct* object of distributive concern. The theory must both treat free time as a discrete component in its distributive metric and realize a just distribution of free time with specifically targeted interventions.

Though the particular policies that are required to address citizens' requirements for time will vary according to the contours of a given theory of

---

Free-Thinker in his *Poor Richard's Almanac* in 1751, but he gave it its fuller and more influential statement in his 1748 letter, in which he writes, "Remember that Time is Money. He that can earn Ten Shillings a Day by his Labour, and goes abroad, or sits idle one half of that Day, tho' he spends but Sixpence during his Diversion or Idleness, ought not to reckon That the only Expence; he has really spent or rather thrown away Five Shillings besides." Franklin's statement of the maxim presages the neoclassical economic conception of time as divided between income-earning labor and income-forgoing leisure, to the effect that one can earn income by spending time or purchase time by forgoing income. See Franklin's letter in *Franklin: The Autobiography and Other Writings on Politics, Economics and Virtue*, ed. Alan Houston (Cambridge: Cambridge University Press, 2004), 200–202.

distributive justice, a range of specifically time-focused policies will generally be required by any theory to ensure that all citizens posses their fair share of free time. While some of the justified policies may deal in the currencies of income and wealth, such as monetary subsidies to caregivers or those with time-intensive disabilities, their justification depends on recognizing and attending to one's share of free time. Moreover, other justified policies, namely institutional labor regulations addressing maximum and flexible hours, overtime work, and family and sick leave, extend beyond the scope of a theory of justice that attends only to the distribution of income and wealth, without any distinct concern for free time. As such, recognizing citizens' distinct claims to free time has significant implications both for theories of distributive justice and for public policy.

Beyond these various time-specific policy measures necessary to ensure that all citizens possess a fair share of free time, there is a further sense in which free time must be treated distinctly. That is, in determining which distributive principle ought to apply to citizens' claims, for instance an egalitarian or sufficientarian principle, some of the relevant considerations apply differently to the resource of free time than to the resources of income and wealth. In particular, because inequalities in free time are less publicly transparent than inequalities in income and wealth, because there are greater natural limits to how vast inequalities in free time can be, and because inequalities in free time less readily translate into inequalities in social status and power, the social egalitarian reasons to favor distributive equality may apply with less force to free time than to income and wealth. In this respect, then, as well, a theory of distributive justice ought to treat free time distinctly from income and wealth.

4.2 THE EFFECTIVE FREEDOMS PRINCIPLE

Liberalism's core commitment to individual liberty has long been criticized as guaranteeing only an empty kind of freedom.[4] The foundation of this critique is the recognition that if one lacks the conditions necessary to exercise a freedom, one in fact only nominally possesses that freedom: without the requisite means one possesses a *formal* or *legal* freedom but lacks the *real*

---

4 Karl Marx, "On the Jewish Question," in *Karl Marx: Selected Writings*, 46–63.

or *effective* freedom, or one has the freedom but it is of little *worth*.[5] Though there are conceptual differences between these approaches, the core of the critique is the same. That is, as Isaiah Berlin asks, "Without adequate conditions for the use of freedom, what is the value of freedom?"[6]

In response, in part, to this critique—which has its greatest force against "classical liberal" theories—liberal egalitarian (or "high liberal") theories endorse some version of the effective freedoms principle. As Samuel Freeman writes, "A basic tenet of high liberalism is that all citizens, as a matter of right and justice, are to have an adequate share of material means so that they are suitably independent, capable of governing and controlling their lives and taking advantage of their basic liberties and fair opportunities." Without such means, "one's liberties and opportunities are worth little," and so the high liberal tradition endorses some form of distributive transfers "to ensure that everyone's liberties and opportunities are of significant value."[7] It is in the context of this liberal egalitarian consensus that Rawls can contend that any reasonable theory of justice must satisfy the effective freedoms principle.[8]

Despite the broad endorsement of the effective freedoms principle among liberal egalitarian theorists of distributive justice, there is considerable diversity in the form the principle takes within different theories: in its grounds (i.e., why citizens have "a legitimate claim"), in its metric (i.e., in what currency a "share" should be measured), in its conditions (i.e., which claims are "fair"), and in its scope (which "formal liberties and opportunities" must be

5 G. A. Cohen, for instance, uses the language of "effective" vs. "legal" freedom and Philippe Van Parijs the language of "real" vs. "formal" freedom. Cohen, "Freedom and Money," in Cohen, *On the Currency of Egalitarian Justice*, 166–92; Van Parijs, *Real Freedom for All*. John Rawls and Isaiah Berlin articulate the point with a distinction between a liberty and its worth or value. Rawls argues that "the inability to take advantage of one's rights and opportunities as a result of poverty and ignorance, and a lack of means generally," though not a constraint on liberty itself, nonetheless affects the "worth of liberty," and distinguishes between the basic liberties and their "fair value." Rawls, *Theory of Justice*, rev. ed., 179.

6 Isaiah Berlin, "Two Concepts of Liberty," in *Liberty* ed. Henry Hardy (1958; repr., Oxford: Oxford University Press, 2002), 171.

7 Samuel Freeman, "Illiberal Libertarians: Why Libertarianism Is Not a Liberal View," *Philosophy & Public Affairs* 30 (2001): 117–18.

8 All liberal egalitarian theories endorse the effective freedoms principle, but it is not exclusive to them. It can be found in a recognizable form in, for instance, Philip Pettit's theory of republicanism, which holds that justice requires that citizens have "equality in the enjoyment of certain fundamental choices, the basic liberties, on the basis of a guarantee of public resources and protections." Pettit, *On the People's Terms: A Republican Theory and Model of Democracy* (Cambridge: Cambridge University Press, 2012), 77.

made effective). Moreover, some theories recognize the effective freedoms principle directly, while others realize it indirectly as embedded in other principles of the theory.[9] The many variations in the principle do not generally bear on the present argument, with two exceptions.

The first point of variation regarding the effective freedoms principle relevant to the present analysis is the question of which formal freedoms citizens have a legitimate claim to enjoying as effective freedoms. Van Parijs's theory of real libertarianism, for instance, offers an expansive view: each citizen has a claim to the effective freedom "to do whatever one might want to do." On this view, no particular liberties or opportunities are selected as those to which citizens have a claim to the requisite resources.[10] Elizabeth Anderson, by contrast, offers a more restricted position: what citizens owe each other, she argues, "are not the means to generic freedoms but the social conditions of the particular, concrete freedoms that are instrumental to life in relations of equality with others." Instead of providing citizens with the means required to exercise what she describes as "optional freedoms," citizens have a legitimate claim only to the resources required to participate as an equal citizen in a democratic state and to participate as an equal in civil society.[11] Because free time is required, as will be clear, on both the more restrictive and expansive views, I will generalize from these two positions to argue that free time is required both to exercise many of one's fundamental freedoms and to pursue one's conception of the good, whatever it may be.

The second relevant point of variation within the literature is the question of which claims to resources are legitimate. Because guaranteeing all citizens the resources they require to exercise their formal freedoms inevitably involves costs to other citizens, if a claim would impose unnecessary or undue costs, satisfying it may be unfair to other citizens. A theory can take a range of positions on the scope of responsibility in qualifying citizens' legitimate claims, and the concepts of choice and responsibility both require further explication on any view, but, put simply, a maximally "responsibility-sensitive"

9 Across different theories, the principle may be read as shorthand for the position that social institutions ought to be arranged, insofar as is possible consistent with the other requirements of justice, such that all citizens have a fair share of the resources generally required to exercise their formal liberties and opportunities. What constitutes a fair share requires further determination, as I discuss in 7.2.

10 Van Parijs, *Real Freedom for All*, 20.

11 Elizabeth Anderson, "Optional Freedoms," in *What's Wrong with a Free Lunch?*, ed. Joshua Cohen and Joel Rogers (Boston: Beacon, 2001), 70–71; "What Is the Point of Equality?," 315–18.

theory holds that any claim to a good or resource, for the lack of which a citizen is herself responsible, is unfair.

There are multiple ways that a theory's responsibility-sensitivity might interact with free time, given that, as noted in 3.8, individuals can make choices that affect how much time it takes to meet their basic needs. Two choices are, however, particularly salient, both because they can each significantly affect how much free time one has and because they are commonly disputed choices within the responsibility literature: that is, one's choice of occupation and one's choice to have procreative children.

First, say one chooses to work at a job that pays low wages when one could readily work at a job that pays much more. If one has less free time on account of working in the low-paying job because one must work longer hours to meet one's basic needs, does one have a legitimate claim to the provision of more free time, or would the satisfaction of such a claim be unfair given that one could have had (and could still have) more free time if one chose the higher paying job? Second, say one has no caregiving obligations and then intentionally chooses to have children. Again, if one has little free time on account of having to care for one's children, does one have a legitimate claim to the provision of free time, or would the satisfaction of such a claim be unfair given that one could have had more free time if one had chosen not to have children?

So that the core argument applies to theories that take a range of positions on responsibility-sensitivity, I draw on cases in which individuals do not lack free time as a result of their choices, so they apply to theories that take both more maximal and more minimal positions on responsibility-sensitivity. Accordingly, the arguments I offer rely on cases in which one works at one's maximum earning capacity and cases in which one does unpaid caregiving for one's infirm parent.[12] When the details of the arguments diverge in significant ways depending on the position a theory takes on responsibility, I present both lines of argument, without endorsing one position over another.

However, after establishing the core argument with these demanding conditions, I do later take positions on these two questions. Specifically, in 6.4, I argue that parents are entitled to public support for producing a public good and so basic child care ought to be treated as a necessary activity,

---

12 Recall from 3.8 that, though one does such caregiving voluntarily, it ought to be treated as a necessary activity because it is the performance of a general social obligation to meet the basic needs of those who are unable to.

and thus as a subtraction from rather than a use of one's free time. Furthermore, at the close of this chapter, in 4.7, I assume for the later chapters that, consistent with the value of freedom of occupational choice, citizens have pro tanto claims to free time within their chosen occupations.

4.3 FREE TIME TO EXERCISE ONE'S FREEDOMS

The effective freedoms principle applies to the resources citizens require in toto, yet the various measures that theories of distributive justice prescribe to satisfy the principle often attend exclusively to the resources of income and wealth. Samuel Freeman's description of the effective freedoms principle as a basic tenet of high liberalism, quoted above, is indicative of this narrow focus: "Without sufficient *income and wealth*, one's liberties and opportunities are worth little. . . . To ensure that everyone's liberties and opportunities are of significant value, the high liberal tradition envisions nonmarket transfers of *income and wealth*."[13]

But, just as someone who lacks the requisite material resources possesses only a formal freedom, so too does someone who lacks the requisite *temporal* resources—that is, the requisite free time. Someone who must spend all of her time satisfying her basic needs does not have the time to take advantage of many of the liberties and opportunities that she formally possesses. An absence of free time constitutes a lack of means in the same way as an absence of income and wealth, and the lack of either renders one less able to take advantage of one's formal liberties and opportunities. Thus, I argue, if a theory of distributive justice endorses the principle that citizens have a legitimate claim to a fair share of the resources generally required to exercise their formal freedoms, then the theory ought to hold that citizens have a legitimate claim to a fair share of free time, because the resource of discretionary time is, parallel to the resources of income and wealth, an all-purpose means generally required to exercise one's formal liberties and opportunities.

Citizens, for instance, generally require free time to exercise their political liberties just as they require income and wealth. Consider an unpaid public office. Since the office is unremunerated, in order to serve in one of these positions one must have enough personal wealth to support oneself for the term of one's position. Thus, those without sufficient wealth have the legal

13 Freeman, "Illiberal Libertarians," 117–18, emphasis added.

right to serve in office, but this right is of little value to them. Consider in addition a public office that is unpaid but part-time: say, a position on one's town school board, for which one has to attend a four-hour meeting once per week. Someone who must work long hours to earn enough money to provide for her and her dependents' basic needs and who must devote extensive time to caregiving does not have the requisite time to serve on the school board. Just as in the case of someone who lacks the requisite personal wealth to serve in office, she too lacks the means to serve in office—the only relevant difference is that the "means" she lacks is time rather than money. She has the freedom to serve in office in a formal sense, but she does not actually enjoy the value of that freedom. This holds true not only for her freedom to serve in office, but for her freedom to run for office, to assemble, to engage in party politics, even to vote.[14]

I highlight how the exercise of the political liberties generally requires free time in particular because of the liberties' priority within many theories of distributive justice, as well as because the example serves to illustrate the way in which citizens generally require free time to exercise any of their formal freedoms. It is worth emphasizing, however, that though I take the political liberties as exemplary, citizens generally require free time for the exercise of all of the basic liberties, and more broadly for any of their formal liberties and opportunities.

4.4 REJECTING THE TIME-MONEY SUBSTITUTABILITY CLAIM

If a given theory of distributive justice endorses, as almost all liberal egalitarian theories do, the effective freedoms principle, and if free time is properly understood as such a resource, then it may seem readily to follow that such a theory must hold that citizens have a legitimate claim to a fair share

---

14 Indeed, though the way an absence of free time can diminish the value of one's political liberties is rarely noted, it is implicitly acknowledged in the common legal requirements that employers give employees time off to vote in elections or to serve on juries. More extensive policies with similar justifications might include paid holidays for public service and political participation. See Stephen Macedo et al., *Democracy at Risk: How Political Choices Undermine Civic Participation, and What We Can Do About It* (Washington, DC: Brookings Institution Press, 2005), 55–56.

of free time and that, therefore, the theory must treat free time as a distinct object of distributive justice.

The final conclusion of the argument does not, however, follow so easily, for it is open to a potential objection: the time-money substitutability claim. True, one might grant that insofar as a theory holds the first two premises—that citizens are entitled to the resources required to exercise their freedoms and that free time is such a resource—it must also hold that citizens have a legitimate claim to free time. But, one might object, this does not necessarily entail that free time must be treated as a *distinct* object of distributive justice. Instead, so the objection presses, a theory of distributive justice could attend solely to the distribution of income and wealth—without any discrete evaluation of or specific provision for free time—and still effectively satisfy citizens' claims to free time. If the time-money substitutability claim were true—if realizing a just distribution of income and wealth is sufficient to ensure a just distribution of free time—then it would not be necessary to treat free time as a distinct object of distributive justice.

It may not be obvious how ensuring that all citizens have a fair share of income and wealth could also ensure that all citizens have a fair share of free time, so to see the force of the objection consider the following example. Say that A must work sixty hours per week to earn enough money to meet her financial basic needs of twenty-five thousand dollars per year at her wage rate of eight dollars per hour.[15] She has a significant commute to work every day because she cannot afford to live near her place of employment, and she must spend a considerable amount of time engaged in the activities necessary to maintain herself and her home because she cannot afford many of the available time-saving conveniences (in-house laundry, prepared foods, household maintenance services, and so on). All told, she has only twenty hours of free time per week. Say that, according to the given theory of distributive justice, A's fair share of free time is fifty hours per week. A, therefore, has an unfair share of free time, with a deficiency of thirty hours per week.

Now, say that the given theory of distributive justice holds that citizens are entitled to a fair share of income and wealth *conditional* on one's willingness to work, and that the modal way of ensuring that all citizens receive

15 At a wage rate of $8 per hour, she actually earns only $24,960 per year, but assume she receives an annual bonus of $40 for simplicity's sake.

their fair share of income and wealth is through wage subsidies. If the given theory of justice prescribes that in order to ensure that A receives her fair share of income and wealth, she is entitled to a wage subsidy of eight dollars per hour, post-subsidy she effectively earns sixteen dollars per hour. According to the time-money substitutability claim, ensuring that A receives her fair share of income and wealth would also automatically ensure that she enjoys her fair share of free time. Post-subsidy, A meets her financial basic needs by working for half the amount of time she did pre-subsidy, so now she has an additional thirty hours of free time, for a total of fifty hours, or her fair share. Perhaps she decides to work only thirty hours per week, and to use the additional thirty hours of free time for other pursuits. Or perhaps she decides to continue working sixty hours per week, and to use the additional income to purchase the time-saving conveniences she could not afford without the subsidy. Either way, it seems as though A enjoys, post-subsidy, at least fifty hours of free time per week. So, in accordance with the time-money substitutability claim, it seems as though a theory of distributive justice that focuses only on the distribution of income and wealth, without any distinct concern for the distribution of free time, would automatically satisfy A's claim to free time.

This result seems all the more assured if a given theory of distributive justice holds that citizens are entitled to a fair share of income and wealth *unconditionally*—that is, independently of one's ability, willingness, or actual performance of work—and that, as on the standard version of such a theory, citizens receive their fair share of income and wealth with a universal basic income. Say that the basic income is twenty-five thousand dollars annually, so all of A's financial basic needs are met with this unconditional grant. A can now choose not to work at all, to the effect that she has more than sixty additional hours of free time. Or perhaps A decides to continue working, either at the same hours or at reduced hours, and to use the basic income to purchase the time-saving conveniences available on the market, so that she has the additional free time both from not having to work and from meeting her other basic needs in less time. Again, either way, the basic income alone seems to ensure that A has a fair share of free time, and thus, in accordance with the time-money substitutability claim, it seems that solely by ensuring that all citizens receive their fair share of income and wealth, without any independent concern for free time, a theory of distributive justice nonetheless automatically also ensures that all citizens have a fair share of free time.

The time-money substitutability claim depends on the assumption that money and time are fungible goods. In the example of A, on both types of theories of distributive justice (work-conditional and work-unconditional), what gives the objection its force is the assumption that A could readily translate the increase in her income to an increase in her free time. The wage subsidy and the basic income can effectively address A's deficiency of free time only insofar as they allow her to either reduce her work hours or to purchase the provision of other necessary activities. As such, the time-money substitutability claim rests on two particular claims about the functioning of economic markets: the perfect divisibility of labor demand and the perfect substitutability of money and basic needs satisfaction.

I argue that neither of these claims can be sustained. I will treat the assumptions in turn as they apply differently to work-conditional and to work-unconditional theories: first, the perfect divisibility of labor demand, which, if invalid, is most problematic for a work-conditional theory; and second, the perfect substitutability of money and basic needs satisfaction, which, though troubling for both, if invalid is more significant for the problems it poses to a work-unconditional theory. Ultimately I argue that neither a work-conditional nor a work-unconditional theory of distributive justice can, by ensuring that all citizens have a fair share of income and wealth, also reliably ensure that all citizens have a fair share of free time. Accordingly, the time-money substitutability claim must be rejected, and thus to ensure that all citizens have their fair shares of both free time and income and wealth, free time must be treated as a distinct object of distributive justice.

The Imperfect Divisibility of Labor Demand

The first assumption on which the time-money substitutability claim depends is the perfect divisibility of labor demand: all individuals can freely choose to reduce their hours of paid work to the level they prefer. If A, for instance, receives a wage subsidy so that she earns sixteen dollars per hour instead of eight, so the claim holds, she would automatically have her fair share of free time because she could satisfy her financial basic needs by working only thirty hours per week, instead of sixty. Yet, A would have her fair share of free time only if she could actually reduce her hours of work from sixty per week to thirty. If she could not reduce her hours—if, for instance, her employer refused to employ her at fewer than sixty hours per week—her higher wage rate would have no effect on how many hours of free time she had (holding her means of satisfying her other basic needs constant for now). She would enjoy a higher income, but she would still suffer from a deficiency of free time.

The assumption that individuals can freely choose to reduce their hours of paid work is thus crucial to the time-money substitutability claim. This assumption is supported by the standard neoclassical economic theory of labor supply, according to which workers can freely choose how many hours to work at a given wage rate. Yet, there is ample empirical evidence suggesting that most workers in fact have limited discretion over how many hours they work. Survey data show that a significant portion of workers would prefer to work fewer hours than they do. In the United States, for instance, recent studies show that between 35 and 65 percent of American workers would prefer to work fewer hours than they actually do. Moreover, of those who would prefer to work fewer hours, the vast majority would prefer to work at least ten hours less per week.[16]

That many workers report that they would prefer to work fewer hours is not in itself conclusive evidence that workers cannot freely reduce their hours of work, as they may be able to reduce their hours of work but be unwilling to accept any corresponding loss of income. What more decisively shows that workers cannot freely reduce their hours of work is evidence that workers would prefer to work fewer hours with the corresponding reduction in income but cannot find employment on these terms in their given occupation. The economic term for this phenomenon is overemployment: workers are overemployed if they would prefer to reduce their hours of work for a proportional reduction in income in their given occupation, but are unable to do so. Estimates of overemployment are somewhat difficult to attain as they depend on counterfactual information, but surveys have measured its occurrence by asking workers if they would prefer to work fewer hours for some corresponding reduction in pay. These studies find that, in

16 Marin Clarkberg and Phyllis Moen, "Understanding the Time-Squeeze: Married Couples' Preferred and Actual Work-Hour Strategies," *American Behavioral Scientist* 44 (2001): 1115–36; Jacobs and Gerson, *Time Divide*, 64; Jeremy Reynolds, "You Can't Always Get the Hours You Want: Mismatches between Actual and Preferred Work Hours in the U.S.," *Social Forces* 81 (2003): 1171–99; Reynolds, "In the Face of Conflict: Work-Life Conflict and Desired Work Hour Adjustments," *Journal of Marriage and Family* 67 (2005): 313–31.

the United States for instance, between 20 and 30 percent of workers are overemployed.[17]

Studies of the labor market confirm what the survey results suggest: that workers have limited discretion over how many hours they engage in paid work and that it is particularly difficult for workers to reduce their work hours. Most employers offer employment only on terms that require all employees to work a certain minimum number of hours per day and/or per week, to the effect that individual workers generally cannot negotiate hours that deviate from this minimum.[18] Nor do workers have significant latitude in reducing their hours by switching employers.[19] Employment in a given occupational category is typically offered only within a range of standard hours, such that workers cannot find an employer willing to hire them for hours below this range.[20] Furthermore, even within the range of hours offered, jobs with longer hours are typically oversupplied and jobs with shorter hours undersupplied, relative to workers' stated preferences. In many occupational categories there are more workers willing to take shorter-hour jobs, even at the correspondingly discounted wage rates, than are available.[21]

Economic theory that improves on the simple model of labor supply to offer a more nuanced understanding of the labor market supports these empirical findings, and indicates that there is reason to believe these constraints would remain under otherwise just background conditions. In brief, three dynamics shaping labor demand may reduce workers' abilities to reduce their work hours. First, there are costs of employment that vary in proportion with the number of workers rather than the number of work hours.

17 Golden and Gebreselassie, "Overemployment Mismatches."

18 Joseph G. Altonji and Christina H. Paxson, "Labor Supply Preferences, Hours Constraints, and Hours-Wages Trade-offs," *Journal of Labor Economics* 6 (1988): 254–76; Maite Martinez-Granado, "Testing Labour Supply and Hours Constraints," *Labour Economics* 12 (2005): 321–43.

19 Workers may be able to adjust their hours by switching occupations, which may or may not be relevant on different theories of justice depending on how sensitive they are to responsibility.

20 Lonnie Golden, "The Economics of Worktime Length, Adjustment, and Flexibility: A Synthesis of Contributions from Competing Models of the Labor Market," *Review of Social Economy* 54 (1996): 1–45; Antonia Díaz and Cristina Echevarria, "Why a Fixed Workweek?" *Journal of Socio-Economics* 38 (2009): 790–98; Jeremy Reynolds and Lydia Aletraris, "Pursuing Preferences: The Creation and Resolution of Work Hour Mismatches," *American Sociological Review* 71 (2006): 618–38.

21 James B. Rebitzer and Lowell J. Taylor, "Do Labor Markets Provide Enough Short Hour Jobs? An Analysis of Work Hours and Work Incentives," *Economic Inquiry* 33 (1995): 257–73.

These fixed labor costs impose a floor on the minimum number of hours for which it is feasible for a firm to hire a worker. They also incentivize employers to prefer maximizing hours per worker, up until the point of diminished productivity. Other costs of employment likewise incentivize firms to prefer employing all workers for the same standard, minimum number of hours.[22] Second, when it is difficult for employers to observe worker productivity, employers use length of work hours as a proxy for productivity and base recruitment, hiring, and promotion decisions on whether workers will or do work long hours. This incentivizes workers to work longer hours and leads to a "rat race" among workers who steadily increase their work hours.[23] Third, under some conditions, employers may pay workers above-market wages because these "efficiency wages" make the loss of the job more costly to workers and, thereby, induce better work performance. Efficiency wages are most effective when the gap between the worker's income from her present job and her next best offer is greatest, and this may incentivize firms to employ workers for maximal hours as a way to widen this gap. Efficiency wages are also most effective with workers who prefer more income to shorter work hours, so firms may use the length of a worker's preferred hours to screen out workers who have a high utility for free time.[24] Together these dynamics lead to the undersupply of shorter-hour jobs and the oversupply of longer-hour jobs.

The time-money substitutability claim depends, in part, on the assumption of perfect divisibility of labor demand. If a worker cannot reduce her hours of work—if neither her current nor a prospective employer is willing to hire her for fewer hours than she presently works—then providing her with a wage subsidy does not actually affect how much free time she has. A work-conditional theory of distributive justice that ensures a fair distribution of income and wealth through wage subsidies or some other work-sensitive

22 Robert A. Hart, *The Economics of Overtime Working* (Cambridge: Cambridge University Press, 2004), 46, 92; Schor, *Overworked American*, 66–68; François Contensou and Radu Vranceanu, *Working Time: Theory and Policy Implications* (Cheltenham: Edward Elgar, 2000), 71.

23 Renée M. Landers, James B. Rebitzer, and Lowell J. Taylor, "Rat Race Redux: Adverse Selection in the Determination of Work Hours in Law Firms," *American Economic Review* 86 (1996): 329–48; Alfonso Sousa-Poza and Alexandre Ziegler, "Asymmetric Information about Workers' Productivity as a Cause for Inefficient Long Working Hours," *Labour Economics* 10 (2003): 727–47.

24 Schor, *Overworked American*, 60–66; Rebitzer and Taylor, "Do Labor Markets Provide Enough Short Hour Jobs?"

means, without any distinct concern for the distribution of free time, cannot, accordingly, also reliably ensure a fair distribution of free time.

Rejecting the perfect divisibility of labor demand is therefore, in itself, decisive to defeat the time-money substitutability claim for any work-conditional theory of distributive justice. Moreover, rejecting this assumption may hold against the claim for a work-unconditional theory as well, depending on the exact contours of the theory. At this juncture, however, two points are clear: first, the assumption of the perfect divisibility of labor demand cannot be sustained; and second, as a result, the time-money substitutability claim does not hold for any work-conditional theory of distributive justice.

The Imperfect Substitutability of Money and Basic Needs Satisfaction

For both work-conditional and work-unconditional theories, the time-money substitutability claim also depends on the remaining assumption: the perfect substitutability of money and basic needs satisfaction. One's free time is not constrained only by the time when one is meeting one's financial basic needs with paid work, but also when one is meeting one's household and bodily basic needs. In addition, one may have caregiving obligations—such as for an infirm parent or spouse or, if relevant on a given theory, for one's children—which also subtract from one's free time. As a result of differences in caregiving obligations, household arrangements (e.g., single or partners, single or dual earners), and bodily demands (e.g., variations in sleep and exercise requirements, disabilities), some individuals may require more time than others to meet their own and their dependents' household and bodily basic needs. If the time one spends engaged in such necessary activities reduces one's free time below the level of one's fair share, then, in order for the time-money substitutability claim to hold, all of one's bodily, household, and caregiving basic needs must be satisfiable through the expenditure of money. The time-money substitutability claim, thus, depends on the further assumption that all individuals can unobjectionably meet their household and bodily basic needs by purchasing goods or services in the marketplace.

The role of this assumption is most apparent and significant in a work-unconditional theory of distributive justice with a universal basic income. Proponents of a basic income generally acknowledge that the level of the basic income would likely be somewhere below subsistence, but to evaluate the time-money substitutability claim in its strongest form, assume that the basic income is equal to the standard level of financial basic need in the society.

To take another example, say that B works thirty hours per week and earns twenty-five thousand dollars per year, enough to meet her financial basic needs. B suffers from arthritis, and though her illness does not debilitate her, it does require management; she must spend twenty hours per week doing physical therapy, administering treatments, and attending medical appointments. B also helps to care for her elderly mother who lives next door—she prepares her meals, helps her bathe, cleans her home, and does her errands, all told for thirty hours per week. When one accounts for the time B must spend sleeping and tending to her own bodily and household basic needs, B has only ten hours of free time per week. Say that, again, B's fair share of free time is fifty hours per week. B, therefore, has an unfair share of free time, with a deficiency of forty hours per week.

Now say that an unconditional basic income is instituted, at the standard level of financial basic need in B's society, twenty-five thousand dollars per year. B could now decide not to work, as the basic income would allow her to meet her financial basic needs without working. This significantly increases her free time—from ten hours per week to forty—but she still has a deficiency, since her fair share is fifty hours. Before proceeding, it is worth noting that, at this point, even the generous work-unconditional income grant, determined and provided without reference to free time, cannot ensure B her fair share of free time, so the time-money substitutability claim apparently cannot be sustained. But, perhaps, one could respond that, if the example stops there, the claim is false, but if further adjustments are made, it is true: that is, if B were to continue working and to use the basic income to meet her household and bodily basic needs, or if B's mother were to use her own basic income to satisfy her own household and bodily basic needs, then the provision of a basic income could automatically and effectively ensure that B has her fair share of free time. As these possible adjustments suggest, the time-money substitutability claim then depends on assuming the perfect substitutability of money and basic needs satisfaction.

This assumption is, however, unsupportable. First, for some necessary activities, it is straightforwardly false. There is (at present) no way one can exchange income for the necessary time one must spend sleeping, nor meeting many of one's other bodily basic needs. One may pay someone else to assist in, for instance, exercising, eating, or grooming, but this income expenditure does not substitute for all or most of the time one must still spend engaged in these activities oneself. B could not, for instance, purchase goods or services to substitute for the time she spends sleeping, engaged in physical therapy, or at the doctor's office. She must unavoidably do these activities herself.

For most people, these bodily basic needs do not make such a demand on one's time so as to result in one having significantly less free time than others, yet for individuals with special needs they may. Providing such individuals with income grants may ensure that they can afford special equipment or assistance, but it cannot substitute for the time they must spend engaged in meeting those bodily basic needs themselves. Thus, ensuring that such individuals have unconditional income grants cannot ensure that they have a fair share of free time. In such cases, money cannot be exchanged for free time.

Second, for a range of other necessary activities, it is indeed true that one *can* substitute income for time engaged in meeting one's household and bodily basic needs—either directly by hiring someone's services or indirectly by purchasing a good—but it does not follow that a theory of justice is entitled to assume that citizens should make such a substitution.

The commodification of household and bodily labor may, under some conditions, indeed be unjust.[25] If market transactions in which one purchases the labor of another to meet one's own household or bodily needs undermine some citizens' equal standing, or the ability of citizens to relate to each other as equals, that commodification may be unjust on account of the threat it poses to civic equality.[26] Though an evaluation of whether such markets would damage citizens' equal standing cannot be made in the abstract, the possibility that such markets may be unjust is enough to prevent the simple assumption that the commodification of household and bodily labor is unproblematic.

Moreover, even if the conditions do not obtain under which such market transactions are unjust, citizens may still have legitimate objections to the commodification of such labor. Citizens may reasonably believe that hiring the services of another to meet their household and caregiving needs may

25 One could go further and argue that paying for caregiving in the home is an "intrinsically unjust practice," as Joan C. Tronto, for instance, does in "The 'Nanny' Question in Feminism," *Hypatia* 17 (2002): 41. I am skeptical that paid domestic caregiving could not, under some conditions, be just, so I advance only the more moderate position that *under some conditions* markets in such goods may be unjust.

26 Satz, *Why Some Things Should Not Be for Sale*, 95.

undermine the personal goods of commitment and intimacy in their relationships, degrade the value of the labor itself, or injure their own personhood.[27] Because citizens may reasonably hold objections of these kinds to commodifying household and bodily labor, it is arguably unacceptable to contend that citizens must be willing to purchase these goods and services instead of performing this labor themselves in order to possess their fair share of free time. Though it is beyond the scope of the present argument to delineate the scope of such legitimate objections, the proponent of the time-money substitutability claim, nonetheless, cannot simply assume that all individuals can unobjectionably meet their household and bodily basic needs by purchasing goods or services.

Thus, even if B could hire someone else to maintain her home and care for her mother, or could purchase prepared foods and other time-saving conveniences, in such a way that she could use her or her mother's basic income to attain her fair share of free time, it cannot simply be assumed that the commodification of such household and bodily labor is unobjectionable. Such commodification may, under some conditions, in fact be unjust, or even if not strictly unjust, B may still have legitimate objections to turning to the market to satisfy these needs.

Therefore, even a work-unconditional theory that provides a generous basic income at the standard level of financial basic need cannot ensure that all citizens have a fair share of free time. Though a work-unconditional theory does not necessarily rely on perfect divisibility of labor demand, it does depend on the perfect substitutability of money and basic needs satisfaction.[28] This assumption, like the first, cannot be sustained, and so the work-unconditional version of the time-money substitutability claim fails as well.

Accordingly, the time-money substitutability claim—that realizing a just distribution of income and wealth is sufficient to ensure a just distribution of free time—cannot be sustained. Achieving a just distribution of income and

27 Elizabeth Anderson, *Value in Ethics and Economics* (Cambridge, MA: Harvard University Press, 1993), 150–58; Michael Sandel, *What Money Can't Buy* (New York: Farrar, Straus and Giroux, 2012), 93–130; Margaret Jane Radin, *Contested Commodities* (Cambridge, MA: Harvard University Press, 1996), 88.

28 If the unconditional basic income is not high enough to meet one's financial basic needs, then the universal grant can ensure that all have a fair share of free time only if, again, they can reduce their hours of work. In such instances, the work-unconditional version of the basic income falls afoul of both assumptions. The same holds true for the work-conditional version, for even if one can reduce one's hours, one can still lack free time by virtue of one's household and bodily basic needs.

wealth cannot reliably guarantee a just distribution of free time. To ensure that citizens possess their fair shares of both income and wealth, and free time, a theory of justice must treat free time as a distinct object of distributive concern.

4.5 DISTINCT DISTRIBUTIVE CONSIDERATIONS

Thus far, I have argued that citizens have legitimate claims to *a fair share* of free time, without specifying what constitutes a fair share. I address this question in full in 7.2, but to preview, the determination of what constitutes a citizen's fair share of free time depends on (1) how much time a society must devote to the shared burdens of social cooperation, (2) which distributive principles apply to citizens' resource claims, (3) the relative weights given to different resources, and (4) whether any special intervening reasons apply to an individual's claim. The second consideration is the focus here, as it highlights another way in which theories of distributive justice ought to treat temporal resources distinctly from material resources. That is, on some distributive theories, there are considerations that tell in favor of applying a different distributive principle to citizens' claims to free time than to their claims to income and wealth.

Within the diverse array of theories that endorse the effective freedoms principle, a range of justifications are offered to ground citizens' claims to the resources they require to exercise their formal freedoms. Some of these justifications require or favor a strictly egalitarian distribution of resources, because they hold that inequality is in itself bad or unjust.[29] Other justifications, however, are consistent with a range of distributive principles, including strict egalitarianism, but also Paretian egalitarianism (all should have the same unless inequalities benefit all), sufficientarianism (all should have enough), or prioritarianism (aiding the worst off should have priority).

When a theory of distributive justice does not hold that distributive inequality is intrinsically bad or unjust, and so does not hold that justice requires distributive equality, a range of other considerations are often invoked to determine the appropriate distributive principle. In this context, a variety of "non-intrinsic" reasons are commonly offered on behalf of an egalitarian

---

29 See Derek Parfit, "Equality or Priority?," in *The Ideal of Equality*, ed. Michael Clayton and Andrew Williams (London: Macmillan, 2000), 81–125.

distribution.[30] These reasons generally derive from the importance distributive equality is taken to have for social equality, that is, for the maintenance of a society in which individuals regard and treat one another as equals.[31] Distributive inequality can threaten social equality by creating and perpetuating stigmatization and status inferiority, objectionable power dynamics, and relations of servility, and by undermining individuals' self-respect and society's sense of community and fraternity.

Whether or not distributive inequality undermines social inequality is, in at least some respects, an empirical question. The assessment of how distributive inequality threatens social inequality is typically made with reference to income and wealth, and it is plain how material inequality could produce these problematic social effects. Even if everyone had some sufficient amount of material resources while a minority had much more, it is not difficult to see how the inequalities could be detrimental to social equality in these ways. Yet, the social egalitarian reasons to favor distributive equality may not apply with the same force to other goods or resources, such that social egalitarianism may be compatible with a different distributive principle, such as sufficientarianism, with respect to some goods or resources. Whether or not these reasons favor distributive equality depends on an assessment specific to the resource in question, and there are, indeed, several ways in which these social egalitarian considerations may apply differently to the resource of free time and the resources of income and wealth.

With respect to these social egalitarian considerations, free time is different from income and wealth in three relevant respects:

First, many of the detrimental effects of wealth inequality on social relations arise because individuals know how much income and wealth others

30 Martin O'Neill, "What Should Egalitarians Believe?," *Philosophy & Public Affairs* 36 (2008): 119–56; T. M. Scanlon, "The Diversity of Objections to Inequality," in Scanlon, *Difficulty of Tolerance*, 202–18. For an account of how a sufficientarian approach can accommodate this range of considerations, see Liam Shields, "The Prospects for Sufficientarianism," *Utilitas* 24 (2012): 101–17.

31 Samuel Scheffler, "What Is Egalitarianism?," *Philosophy & Public Affairs* 31 (2003): 21–24, and "Choice, Circumstance, and the Value of Equality," *Philosophy, Politics & Economics* 4 (2005): 17–23; Elizabeth Anderson, "What Is the Point of Equality?" and "The Fundamental Disagreement between Luck Egalitarians and Relational Egalitarians," *Canadian Journal of Philosophy Supplementary Volume* 36 (2010): 1–23; Norman Daniels, "Democratic Equality: Rawls's Complex Egalitarianism," in Freeman, *Cambridge Companion to Rawls*, 241–76; and T. M. Scanlon, "Rawls' Theory of Justice," *University of Pennsylvania Law Review* 121 (1973): 1056–69.

have. It is because inequalities in wealth are, to some extent, public knowledge that such inequalities lead to stigmatizing differences in social status, damage the self-respect of the worse off, and undermine healthy fraternal social relations. Even if individuals' salaries and net worth are not publicly available, the different lifestyles they permit often telegraph this information. In contrast, how much free time one has is not as readily evident, since some portion of the time one engages in different typically necessary activities may be free time. Two coworkers, A and B, might, for instance, spend the same amount of time engaged in paid work, while A earns twice as much per hour as B does. Assuming that both A and B can choose their hours of work, A accordingly has twice as much free time as B does because she must work for only half as much time as B to meet her basic financial needs. Though B could determine that A has twice as much free time as he does if he knows how much A earns, he is more likely to simply observe that they work the same number of hours. The inequality in their incomes or job titles might be problematic for the reasons identified above, but the inequality in their free time, in particular, is not as likely to be because it is not the same type of immediately apparent public knowledge.

Second, all of the damaging effects of distributive inequality on social relations are likely to be worsened as the degree of inequality increases. In this respect, inequalities in income and wealth can be quite problematic, for there is theoretically no limit to how great the material disparities in a society can be. The richest one percent might earn or own one hundred times as much as the poorest one percent, or one thousand times as much, or one million times as much: there is no natural limit to the potential disparity. The potential for extreme wealth inequality tells strongly against a merely sufficientarian distribution of income and wealth when one is weighing the impact on social equality. It is difficult to imagine that ensuring that all citizens have "enough" wealth, while permitting some citizens to have vastly more than the rest, would not damage equal social relations.

Yet, unlike income and wealth, there *is* a natural limit to inequalities in free time. Setting aside even the presently unavoidable natural limit of time one must spend directly satisfying one's basic needs, time is of course finite and the most free time one could possibly have is twenty-four hours per day. Inequalities of free time would thus be limited to the space between the sufficient level and the upper limit of twenty-four hours per day. Even if one enjoyed complete free time every day of one's life, the resultant inequality between this time-blessed person and those who enjoyed only the minimally sufficient level is more limited than the possible inequalities of income and wealth.[32] While the deleterious effects of inequality might still present themselves with such inequalities of free time—and I do not mean to diminish the problems these inequalities might pose—the effects might still be less pronounced than with the unbounded inequalities of material resources.

Third, material inequalities readily translate into inequalities in other domains. Wealth inequalities can create relations of domination, subordination, and servility in part because one who possesses a greater amount of wealth—or, more specifically, money—can use one's money to buy not only specific goods but also, in effect, power. As Jeremy Waldron writes, "A person who has money can buy a better house, an exotic vacation, a fancy car, and well-tailored clothes; but he can also secure a better education for his children, buy a place in a privately protected community, influence the outcome of an election, change the editorial tone of a newspaper, and endow a university chair."[33] In market economies, money is, in Walzer's phrase, "a dominant good"—those who have it, because they have it, can command a wide range of other goods.[34] Unless constraints are imposed on what one can buy and sell, money readily serves as a dominant good largely because, as the medium of exchange, it is highly fungible with other goods.

Free time, by contrast, is not so readily a dominant good, primarily because it is less fungible with other goods. Though one can use one's free time to attain various goods, such as additional income, education, influence, or accolades, one must use one's free time directly to attain these goods oneself, by spending one's time in the relevant activity. To use one's free time to affect the outcome of an election, or to provide one's children with a better education, or to attain a university chair, one must spend one's time politicking, teaching, or studying. One cannot simply transfer one's free time to someone else in exchange for the desired good. As such, money, in contrast to free time, is a more fungible—and thus more readily dominant—good.

---

32 See Clayne Pope, "Measuring the Distribution of Material Well-Being: U.S. Trends," *Journal of Monetary Economics* 56 (2009): 77.

33 Jeremy Waldron, "Money and Complex Equality," in Miller and Walzer, *Pluralism, Justice, and Equality*, 146.

34 Walzer, *Spheres of Justice*, 12.

For two reasons, however, these dissimilarities between the resource of free time and the resources of income and wealth do not decisively establish that free time ought to be distributed in accordance with some principle other than an egalitarian one. First, as noted, a theory of distributive justice may hold that all resources must be distributed equally, without any regard to the types of concerns about social equality drawn on here; for such a theory, these dissimilarities have no relevance. Second, even for theories of distributive justice that do account for social equality in the determination of distributive principles, whether or not these distinctions would in fact differentially affect social equality is an empirical question, to be evaluated in particular circumstances. Nonetheless, for distributive theories that do rely on social egalitarian considerations, these dissimilarities between material and temporal resources must be taken into account. Accordingly, a theory of distributive justice must, in this way, further consider the resource of free time distinctly from the resources of income and wealth.

4.6 FREE TIME AS A DISTINCT OBJECT OF DISTRIBUTIVE JUSTICE

Treating free time as a distinct object of distributive concern entails two requirements for a theory of justice. First, a theory must recognize free time as a discrete component in its distributive metric. It must evaluate how much time it takes one to meet one's own and one's dependents' basic needs, aggregating across the domains of paid work, household labor, and personal care. A theory of distributive justice must separately consider how much free time citizens possess, rather than relying on how much they possess of the resources of income and wealth as adequate proxies for free time.

Second, a theory must realize a just distribution of free time with specifically targeted provisions. These time-focused policies must ensure that citizens are able to spend, if x is one's fair share of free time, no more than $(24 - x)$ hours per day meeting their basic needs. There are many possible ways to ensure such a just distribution of free time, but, broadly, a theory must include provisions to guarantee, insofar as is possible consistent with the other requirements of justice: (1) that all citizens can in fact *meet* their basic needs in $(24 - x)$ hours per day, and (2) that all citizens can in fact *choose* to spend no more than $(24 - x)$ hours per day meeting their basic needs. Accordingly, two types of time-targeted provisions are generally required: to

(1), those that allow citizens to meet their basic needs in less time so they can have their fair shares of free time (public provisions or income subsidies); and to (2), those that protect citizens' ability to choose to spend no more time meeting their basic needs than is necessary to have their fair shares of free time (regulations). In addition, citizens must possess their shares of free time under conditions that allow them to make effective use of it to exercise their liberties. I examine in greater detail the implications for public policy of recognizing citizens' claims to a fair share of free time in 7.3.

In summary, the exercise of one's formal liberties generally requires the resources of both money and time, and so a theory of distributive justice that endorses the effective freedoms principle, as almost all do, ought to hold that citizens have legitimate claims not only to income and wealth, but also to free time. Yet, existing theories of distributive justice, while giving ample attention to the resources of income and wealth, have nearly entirely ignored the resource of free time. They have done so as they have assumed the time-money substitutability claim: that realizing a just distribution of income and wealth is sufficient to ensure a just distribution of free time. If it were true, the time-money substitutability claim would conveniently simplify our theories of distributive justice. Yet, with regrets to simplicity, the time-money substitutability claim is false: realizing a just distribution of income and wealth cannot reliably guarantee a just distribution of free time. As such, free time must be treated as a distinct object of distributive justice.

4.7 FREE TIME AND OCCUPATIONAL CHOICE

On the basis of the widely held effective freedoms principle, all citizens have legitimate claims to a fair share of free time. This core argument applies, across the many variations in theories of distributive justice, to any theory that endorses the effective freedoms principle. For the following chapters, as I extend the argument, I will take particular positions on two of these points of variation, both with respect to responsibility. In 6.4, I argue that parents' basic caregiving for children ought to be treated as a necessary activity, and thus as a subtraction from one's free time. Here I argue, against the maximally responsibility-sensitive position, that citizens have a pro tanto claim to a fair share of free time within their chosen occupations.

If one did not have a claim to free time within one's chosen occupation, one's claim to free time could be satisfied if a single decent occupational position was available that allowed for free time. This position could be a single occupation at one's maximum earning capacity, or a single occupation provided by the government for this purpose. On this maximally responsibility-sensitive view, if one could have one's fair share of free time only if one chose to be, for instance, a doctor or, alternately, a public works employee, if one chooses any other occupation, one has no claim to free time in that chosen occupation. I take this view to be incompatible with the value of freedom of occupational choice. Freedom of occupation is widely held to be a fundamental liberty, reflecting, in part, the important interest citizens have in choosing their occupations given the centrality of occupation to the pursuit of one's conception of the good.[35] The importance of this interest in occupational choice provides a weighty reason to allow for citizens to exercise this choice without forfeiting their claims to other important interests, including to generally required resources like free time. Citizens ought to have their fair shares of free time within their chosen occupations.

Though one has an all things considered claim to a fair share of free time, one's claim to free time in one's chosen occupation is, however, only a pro tanto claim. This pro tanto claim can be defeated by several types of reasons. First, some occupational positions depend on having relative excellence within a category, a superiority that may not be attainable without working long hours. If this reason applies, one still ought to be entitled to free time within one's occupational category (e.g., lawyer), even if not to free time within a particular occupational position (e.g., lawyer at a particular firm). Second, it might be impossible or prohibitively socially costly to provide those who work in some occupations with free time for reasons particular to that occupation. Some of these reasons relate to the demands or structure of the occupation. For instance, the importance of military discipline might require soldiers to work long hours, or, to take an unusual case, the nature of the job might prevent astronauts from having free time. (Reasons of this type ought to be regarded warily, as most occupations can be reorganized without great social cost to allow for free time, if not daily or weekly, at least in concentrated periods.) Another set of reasons relates to the problems posed by guaranteeing free time. For instance, guaranteeing free time to the self-employed might introduce an unacceptable moral hazard problem. If these types of exceptional reasons apply to a particular occupation, one may

---

35 See Rawls, *Political Liberalism*, 308, 335; *Theory of Justice*, rev. ed., 362–65; and *Justice as Fairness*, 158.

not have a claim to free time within that occupation, though one's claim to free time still applies outside that occupation. Thus, citizens are, all things considered, entitled to a fair share of free time, and furthermore, unless an intervening reason applies, they are entitled to a fair share of free time while working in their chosen occupations.

CHAPTER 5

SHARED FREE TIME

5.1 THE TEMPORAL COORDINATION PROBLEM

Different theories of justice realize the effective freedoms principle in different ways, but there is a general tendency to treat both the liberties and the resources monolithically, with reference simply to "one's liberties and opportunities" and "all-purpose means." While these shorthands are not necessarily problematic when articulating the grounds and value of the effective freedoms principle, they must be disaggregated and examined separately when analyzing the discrete claims the principle grounds. If this analysis is never undertaken, it limits the ability of our theories of justice to recognize and respond to many important problems of social and political life—as with the tendency to consider the requirement for all-purpose means generally, and to equate such means with "income and wealth," and the resulting neglect of citizens' distinct demands for the resource of free time and the attendant labor policies that are required to guarantee citizens access to free time. This kind of mistake obscures the value of the effective freedoms principle. Following the principle from underlying grounds to specific claims to public policy extends the principle's normative and practical reach. This chapter further illustrates this point by focusing on citizens' requirements for shared free time for the exercise of freedom of association.

Like the freedom to vote, the exercise of one's freedom of association—understood broadly as the freedoms of intimate, religious, social, and civic association—generally requires the resources of both money and free time. To associate with one's fellow hobbyists at club meetings, for instance, one generally requires money for club dues and the free time to attend the meeting.[1] Yet, free association also requires something further. It generally requires free time that is *shared* with one's fellow associates. While some aspects of the exercise of freedom of association may be engaged in nonsynchronously (for instance, some forms of communicating or organizing), the central exercises of freedom of association must be done synchronously. In order to share a meal with family members, participate in a community event with neighbors, march in a rally with one's political copartisans, play a sport with one's teammates, or share religious services with one's fellow believers, one and one's fellow associates must engage in the pursuit at the same time. In addition to the all-purpose resources of money and free time, *effective freedom of association*, I argue, requires that one has reasonable access to sufficient periods of free time shared with a significant portion of those with whom one currently associates and might associate.

Potential associates face a constant challenge, which we may call the *temporal coordination problem*: potential associates must synchronize their schedules to realize periods of shared free time. The temporal coordination problem is pervasive; it arises whenever potential associates attempt to find shared periods of free time. If citizens can in fact coordinate their time such that they do have reasonable access to sufficient periods of shared free time, the temporal coordination problem does not undermine effective freedom of association. Under some circumstances, however, the temporal coordination problem is difficult enough to solve that it does deny some citizens effective freedom of association. As such, on the grounds of the effective freedoms principle, social institutions ought to be arranged—insofar as it is possible consistent with the other principles of justice—such that the temporal coordination problem does not deny citizens effective freedom of association.

The circumstances of contemporary liberal societies, with large, diverse populations and limited amounts of free time, arguably render the temporal coordination problem difficult enough for some citizens to solve that they do lack effective freedom of association. I consider three possible ways a society could address the temporal coordination problem: guaranteeing citizens vast amounts of free time, guaranteeing employees work hours flexibility, and instituting a common period of free time. Which solution is best depends on empirical social circumstances and on the weights given to other

1 Importantly, one also generally requires access to physical space, either public or private, to exercise associational liberties, another resource that has been relatively neglected.

principles and values in a theory of justice. Under different empirical and normative conditions, any of these solutions, or some combination of them, or perhaps some other solution, may be best.

Unlike the other two, however, the third solution—a common period of free time—has long existed in many societies, including in modern liberal democracies in the form of Sunday closing laws, and for this reason this possible solution warrants particular consideration.

The argument proceeds as follows. I begin by establishing the importance of shared free time for effective freedom of association, and the difficulty posed by the temporal coordination problem. I then, in the third section, present three possible solutions to the temporal coordination problem. The argument pauses, in the fourth section, to consider Sunday closing laws' religious origins and their secular purposes as identified by the U.S. Supreme Court. Resuming the argument in the fifth section, I argue that a common period of Sunday free time, if properly justified and instituted, does further effective freedom of association and is consistent with standard liberal egalitarian principles. I conclude by noting that this case illustrates how analyzing and applying the effective freedoms principle in a disaggregated fashion— assessing the particular resources that are required for particular liberties— enhances the principle's range and value.

5.2 EFFECTIVE FREEDOM OF ASSOCIATION AND SHARED FREE TIME

It is plain upon a moment's reflection that citizens generally require shared periods of free time in order to associate. The central exercises of freedom of association, whether intimate, religious, social, or civic, depend on sharing free time together. Though associations are often facilitated by nonsynchronous activities (e.g., organizing and communicating) and some associations may consist entirely in nonsynchronous exchanges (e.g., an epistolary friendship), associations generally depend on spending time together. Whether with one's family and friends, one's fellow hobbyists or enthusiasts, one's fellow partisans or activists, or one's fellow believers, one and one's fellow associates must generally engage in their associational activity at the same time.[2]

---

2 As the sociologist Christopher Winship puts it, "Scheduling conflicts are potentially important barriers to the enactment of social relations. . . . Conflicts affect the potential for

The importance of shared free time for free association is well illustrated with an extreme—but historical rather than hypothetical—example. For two years, from 1929 to 1931, the Soviet Union experimented with replacing the traditional seven-day week with a common day of rest, with a five-day week with staggered rest days. Under the new time regime, economic production was maintained continuously, with each day being a rest day for one-fifth of the society. Individuals were assigned to different rest-day cohorts, with little regard for splitting families or other associational ties. The state "essentially divided the entire society into five separate working populations, staggered vis-à-vis one another like the different voices in a polyphonic, five-voice fugue."[3] The consequence was that members of each rest-day cohort could generally associate only with members of the same rest-day cohort, and as a result, the society's associational life—political, social, and familial—diminished. As one citizen complained at the time the new week was introduced, "What is there for us to do at home if our wives are in the factory, our children at school, and nobody can visit us . . . ? It is no holiday if you have to spend it alone."[4] In 1931, due to the absence of anticipated economic gains, as well as perhaps the significant social discontent, the Soviet Union reinstated a common day of rest.[5]

While Soviet citizens had the opportunity to associate with those in their rest-day cohort under the staggered rest-day regime, they could not maintain their preexisting associations or forge new associations with those assigned to different rest days. The value of freedom of association depends on having the opportunity to both maintain existing ties and to create new ones. Effective freedom of association, then, does not merely require that one has access to some fellow citizens with whom one might associate. It requires that one has opportunity to both continue existing associations and to form new ones, or, to use Robert Putnam's language, to engage in both bonding and bridging associations.[6]

---

certain types of groups to exist." Winship, "Time and Scheduling," in *The Oxford Handbook of Analytical Sociology*, ed. Peter Hedström and Peter Bearman (Oxford: Oxford University Press, 2009), 499.

3 Eviatar Zerubavel, *The Seven Day Circle: The History and Meaning of the Week* (1985; repr., Chicago: University of Chicago Press, 1989), 38.

4 Quoted in ibid., 38.

5 Clive Foss, "Stalin's Topsy-Turvy Work Week," *History Today* 54 (2004): 46–47; Rakoff, *Time for Every Purpose*, 34–55; Zerubavel, *Seven Day Circle*, 35–43.

6 Robert D. Putnam, *Bowling Alone: The Collapse and Revival of American Community* (New York: Simon & Schuster, 2000). It is perhaps worth stressing that the argument for effective

Effective freedom of association, then, requires that one has a fair share of free time shared with a significant portion of those with whom one currently associates and might associate. Given that what constitutes a fair share can be specified differently according to different accounts of distributive justice, as I discuss in 7.2, to proceed with the argument, I will use the less demanding formulation of reasonable access to sufficient periods of shared free time.[7]

Free association always faces, to some degree, the temporal coordination problem. Under some conditions, the temporal coordination problem may be easy enough to overcome that it does not threaten effective freedom of association. On this account, if it is possible for one, with moderate effort, to resolve the temporal coordination problem to the extent that one does have sufficient periods of shared free time with enough of one's current and potential associates, then the existence of the temporal coordination problem does not render one without effective freedom of association. Yet, if these conditions do not obtain, the temporal coordination problem does undermine one's effective freedom of association.

The temporal coordination problem is exacerbated by at least three social circumstances: (1) the diversity of a society's population, as in a more diverse society each citizen has a broader set of potential associations and citizens' sets of associations could overlap less, (2) the amount of free time citizens have, as less free time diminishes the potential shared free time, and (3) the proportion of citizens with nonstandard work schedules, as such schedules reduce the scope of potential shared free time.

To speak to the empirical extent of the third factor, in the contemporary United States, for instance, only one-third of employed Americans work the "standard" thirty-five- to forty-hour, Monday to Friday daytime work schedule. When the hours condition is removed, it is still only a bare majority

---

freedom of association does not rely on the perfectionist judgment that an associational life is better or more worthwhile than a non-associational one. The argument depends on the non-perfectionist commitment to ensuring that citizens enjoy the value of their liberties, that is, that they possess the resources generally required to exercise their freedoms, if they so choose.

7 To elaborate on the qualifications, effective freedom of association requires *reasonable*, not guaranteed, access to periods of shared free time, in that one must have access only under standard (not exceptional) circumstances and with a moderate degree of effort (not with either no effort or great effort). It requires access to only *sufficient* periods of shared free time, with sufficiency determined by the end of maintaining and creating associations and set at some minimal threshold. And it requires access to a *significant portion* of one's current and potential associates, not access to all or only some of either.

that work the standard weekly daytime schedule. As noted in 1.4, over one-third of employed Americans regularly work one or both weekend days, with 8 percent working seven days per week. On a typical day, over one-quarter of American employees perform some work between ten in the evening and six in the morning. Of employed Americans, 8 percent regularly work evenings, 4 percent regularly work nights, and another 8 percent have variable or rotating work schedules. In one-fourth of dual-earner married couples, one or both spouses work non-daytime or rotating shifts. Around one-quarter of employed Americans face mandatory overtime work.[8]

These nonstandard work schedules, both for those who have them and for those who currently associate or might associate with those who have them, make it more difficult for current and potential associates to find shared free time. Most social, recreational, and civic gatherings occur around the standard workweek, on evenings and weekends. Both employed *and* unemployed Americans spend far more time socializing with family members and friends on Saturdays and Sundays than the other days of the week. Those who work these days have less opportunity to spend time with family members, friends, colleagues, and neighbors, and time-use research indicates that their diminished social time on the weekends is not offset with time off on other days of the week. As such, it has become common to describe nonstandard schedules as "unsociable" work hours.[9]

5.3 THREE POSSIBLE SOLUTIONS

For citizens in diverse liberal societies who have little free time and who have nonstandard work schedules, the temporal coordination problem may be difficult enough to solve that they lack effective freedom of association. Insofar as it is possible, consistent with the other principles of justice, social institutions ought to be arranged such that the temporal coordination prob-

---

8 Hamermesh and Stancanelli, "Long Workweeks and Strange Hours," 1009–10; Presser, *Working in a 24/7 Economy*, 15–17; Presser, "Employment Schedules among Dual-Earner Spouses and the Division of Household Labor by Gender," *American Sociological Review* 59 (1994): 357; Golden and Wiens-Tuers, "Mandatory Overtime Work in the United States," 9.

9 Michael Bittman, "Sunday Working and Family Time," *Labour & Industry* 16 (2005): 59, 75–76, which shows that "as compared to those who work on weekdays, Sunday workers miss out on key types of social participation." See also Cristobal Young and Chaeyoon Lim, "Time as a Network Good: Evidence from Unemployment and the Standard Workweek," *Sociological Science* 1 (2014): 10–27.

lem does not deny citizens effective freedom of association, so all citizens have their legitimate claims to reasonable access to sufficient periods of shared free time.

There may be many ways that social institutions could be arranged to address the temporal coordination problem and provide effective freedom of association, but three readily identifiable candidates for diverse liberal societies are guaranteeing citizens vast amounts of free time, guaranteeing employees work hours flexibility, and instituting a common period of free time. The first addresses the second exacerbating factor to the temporal coordination problem, the lack of free time, and the other two address the third factor, nonstandard work schedules.

These policy solutions are offered not as an exhaustive list, nor as universal or perfect solutions. The principled point is that citizens have legitimate claims to shared free time for effective freedom of association. How best to realize these claims is unavoidably a contingent one, depending on empirical social facts about the size, diversity, associational patterns, workplace arrangements, and resources of the society, and depending on normative considerations about the weights given to other principles or values in a theory of justice. Moreover, it may be that none of these solutions would provide a perfect solution, as it may not be possible to resolve the temporal coordination problem for every citizen. That said, each would serve to further effective freedom of association.

The first solution is to guarantee citizens vast amounts of free time, say, eighty hours of free time per week.[10] The more free time citizens have, ceteris paribus, the more easily they can coordinate periods of shared free time. Guaranteeing citizens vast amounts of free time would reliably ensure that citizens have effective freedom of association, as it would provide citizens with reasonable access to sufficient periods of shared free time. One way to implement this solution would be with a universal basic income set at a level that would allow citizens to either work very few hours or cease working entirely.

The second solution does not increase citizens' fair shares of free time, but instead addresses the inflexibility of some citizens' work schedules by guaranteeing all employees greater discretion over their work hours. By providing

10 This may amount to an entitlement for an able-bodied person without any dependents to spend no more than ten hours per week in paid work, if it is standardly necessary to spend seventy-eight hours per week in personal care and household labor to meet one's basic needs.

citizens with the ability to choose when their free time occurs, the solution aims to give citizens greater ability to choose periods of free time shared with their fellow associates. It would be both difficult and costly to guarantee all employees complete discretion over their individual work schedules, since many employment arrangements depend on employees working either at the same time as other employees (e.g., during "business hours") or at different times from other employees (e.g., in work shifts). A more modest proposal is to guarantee all employees the right to take at least one free day per week on the day of their choosing. While some occupations may require exemptions, such a provision would still increase citizens' abilities to coordinate to find shared periods of free time.

The third solution addresses the problem of nonstandard work hours by universalizing rather than by individualizing free time—that is, by establishing a common period of free time. A common period of free time addresses the temporal coordination problem directly by providing all or most citizens, to the extent possible, with access to a period of shared free time. The common period of free time need not be on any particular day, nor on a single day of the week; it could be divided across days, of a greater duration than one day, or distributed on an irregular (say, holiday) schedule. Furthermore, the common period of free time may be, and likely should be, only a portion of one's entire share of free time. So long as the common period of free time is of sufficient duration, it would provide shared free time for effective freedom of association.

Which of these solutions is the best way to ensure effective freedom of association is necessarily contingent. Under some circumstances, the first solution, guaranteeing citizens vast amounts of free time, may be the best way—that is, the most reliable and with the least cost to other appropriately weighted values—of ensuring effective freedom of association. This solution is not, however, always an option. Sometimes, there may be too much work to be done in a society in order for it to meet its requirements of justice, either domestically or internationally, or a society may not have enough material resources available to fund so much guaranteed free time. And, of course, even if guaranteeing citizens vast amounts of free time were materially viable and consistent with the other requirements of justice, doing so may be politically infeasible.

If the first solution were not an option, due to either material or political infeasibility, the second solution, guaranteeing employees work hours flexibility, may seem to be the next best choice. Yet this increased discretion solution may not be as effective in meeting the temporal coordination problem as it may seem given the nature of citizens' associational lives. Citizens typically have or seek associations with multiple sets of associates, and these multiple sets do not typically fully overlap. One often associates with one set of fellow citizens for political causes, another for religious practices, another for family life, and yet more for social purposes. Not only does this often occur, this diversity of associations is to be welcomed in a pluralistic democratic society. But equipped with the right to choose their day of free time, some citizens may choose Monday free time, some Wednesday, others Friday, as each individual attempts to realize or otherwise prioritize her own associational pursuits. Though one may be able to choose one's own day of rest, one cannot also determine the rest days of one's fellow citizens.

This second solution may be a reliable means of solving the temporal coordination problem, but the third solution, instituting a common period of free time, provides an alternative approach, by establishing a time when all or most members of society are free to associate. Indeed, liberal democratic societies have long had such an institution, in the form of Sunday closing laws, which provided a common period of free time. In the remainder of this chapter, I examine the origins, justifications, and current status of Sunday closing laws, and argue that, if properly justified and instituted, Sunday free time laws do reliably further effective freedom of association and are consistent with standard liberal egalitarian principles. To be clear before proceeding, however, any of these solutions, or some other solution, or some combination of them may, depending on the circumstances, be the best means of providing shared free time for effective freedom of association. My primary aim is to establish that, on the grounds of the effective freedoms principle, citizens do have legitimate claims to shared free time, and that these claims ought to be given their appropriate weight in the evaluation of social institutions.

5.4 SUNDAY CLOSING LAWS

Sunday closing laws, which broadly prohibit labor and commerce on Sundays, plainly have religious roots. Sunday legislation was originally enacted in accordance with God's rest on the seventh day of creation, as Exodus 20:8–10 commands: "Remember the Sabbath Day, to keep it holy. Six days you shall labor, and do all your work, but the seventh day is a Sabbath to the Lord your God."[11] Historically, Sunday closing laws were strongest and most prevalent across the United States and Europe. I focus here on the case of Sunday closing laws in the United States.

American colonial law prohibited Sunday labor explicitly in observance of and to foster the Christian religion. The Pennsylvania Body of Laws of 1682 is representative:

> But to the end That Looseness, irreligion, and Atheism may not Creep in under pretense of Conscience in this Province, *Be It further Enacted . . .* That, according to the example of the primitive Christians, and for the ease of the creation, Every first day of the week, called the Lord's day, People shall abstain from their usual and common toil and labour, That whether Masters, Parents, Children, or Servants, they may the better dispose themselves to read the Scriptures of truth at home, or frequent such meetings of religious worship abroad, as may best sute their respective persuasions.[12]

After the colonial era, most of the new states reenacted their Sunday legislation, removing only provisions requiring church attendance. Despite the apparent conflict with the Establishment Clause of the new Constitution's First Amendment—which holds that "Congress shall make no law respecting an establishment of religion"—the Christian justification for the laws persisted. Indeed, as late as 1934, the Maryland Court of Appeals argued, "Ours is a Christian community, and a day set apart as the day of rest, is the day consecrated by the resurrection of our Saviour, and embraces the twenty-four hours next ensuing the midnight of Saturday."[13]

In the 1961 *McGowan v. Maryland* decision, which still stands, the U.S. Supreme Court ruled on the constitutionality of Sunday closing laws, and by an eight-to-one vote, upheld the laws. The Court argued that, though Sunday restrictions were originally enacted primarily to institutionalize and promote

---

11 Early Christians kept both the Jewish Saturday Sabbath and Sunday as "the Lord's Day," but eventually observed only a Sunday day of rest to distinguish themselves. In 321 CE, Constantine decreed the first Sunday labor law, establishing the Sunday Sabbath as a day of rest. Rakoff, *Time for Every Purpose*, 36–38; Alexis McCrossen, *Holy Day, Holiday: The American Sunday* (Ithaca: Cornell University Press, 2000), 9.

12 David N. Laband and Deborah Hendry Heinbuch, *Blue Laws: The History, Economics, and Politics of Sunday Closing Laws* (Lexington, MA: Lexington Books, 1987), 33.

13 Cited in *McGowan v. Maryland*, 366 U.S. 447.

the Christian faith, they were also instituted in part on secular grounds, and that those secular grounds over time had become the primary justification for the laws. The Court argued that if the religious justification were the sole or even primary present grounds for Sunday labor laws, they would for that reason be unconstitutional. However, the Court's majority and concurring opinions argued that the present legislative justifications for Sunday labor laws are secular not religious and ruled that as such they do not constitute an establishment of religion, and so do not violate the First Amendment's Establishment Clause.[14]

Indeed, the Court cited three primary and distinct secular purposes served by the Sunday regulations: the creation of a community atmosphere of repose, the maintenance of a cultural tradition, and the coordination of citizens' free time.[15] In considering these justifications for Sunday labor laws, the justices took it for granted that legislation guaranteeing all citizens a day of rest is constitutional, whether that rest be on different assigned days or on the day of one's choosing. The central question the justices considered in *McGowan* was not whether the state could "provide a one-day-in-seven work stoppage"— that was assumed—but instead whether, first, the state could prescribe a *common* day of rest and then, secondarily, whether that day of rest could be Sunday.

The first secular justification for Sunday labor laws endorsed by the justices, and emphasized in particular by Chief Justice Earl Warren, is that such laws serve the end of creating "an atmosphere of entire community repose." The laws, Warren argued, "seem clearly to be fashioned for the purpose of providing a Sunday atmosphere of recreation, cheerfulness, repose and enjoyment," to establish "the air of the day" as "one of relaxation," to establish

---

14 In a subsequent 1961 decision, *Braunfeld v. Brown* (366 U.S. 599), the Court held that the laws also do not violate the First Amendment's Free Exercise Clause ("Congress shall make no law . . . prohibiting the free exercise" of religion). See Sonu Bedi, *Rejecting Rights* (Cambridge: Cambridge University Press, 2009), 132.

15 The justices do cite an additional secular justification on behalf of Sunday labor laws, but as neither the majority nor concurring opinions explicitly endorse it, I only note it here. That is, Sunday regulations are, as a 1711 issue of the weekly *Spectator* contends, the "best method . . . for polishing and civilizing of mankind." The Sunday day of rest, as Blackstone wrote in the mid-1700s, "humanizes, by the help of conversation and society, the manners of the lower classes, which would otherwise degenerate into a sordid ferocity and savage selfishness of spirit." *McGowan v. Maryland*, 366 U.S. 477n27 (Frankfurter, J., concurring) and 366 U.S. 434.

"a day on which there exists relative quiet and disassociation from the everyday intensity of commercial activities." The laws aim to "provide for a general cessation of activity, a special atmosphere of tranquility," an atmosphere that Justice Felix Frankfurter argued may be necessary for its "recuperative effects." Though Justice Frankfurter granted that the maintenance of a community atmosphere is "a subtle *desideratum*," he nonetheless maintained that the state's interest in obtaining an atmosphere of quiet repose was legitimate and that the state could reasonably determine that only a universal day of rest could serve that interest.[16]

The second secular justification the justices articulated in support of the Sunday labor laws is that they serve to maintain a cultural tradition. On this view, offered only in Justice Frankfurter's concurrence (which Justice Harlan joined), in instituting Sunday regulations, the state's "purpose is the preservation of a traditional institution." The traditional Sunday, "a cultural asset of importance," carries "special, long established associations." Those associations center not on the day's religious meaning, but on the day as the "recurrent note of repose" in the "hebdomadal rhythm" of life, a "recurrent time in the cycle of human activity" when one departs from the routines of daily life.[17]

In considering these justifications on behalf of Sunday labor laws, the Court held them only to the standard for determining constitutionality. There may be merit to these two justifications, and depending on one's full theory of justice, one might (or might not) find them to be relevant considerations in favor of enacting Sunday closing laws. My aim here is not to evaluate these two justifications, but to draw attention to the third justification. That is, as the justices argued, Sunday closing laws serve to provide citizens with periods of shared free time.

The Court argued that the alternative, a "rest one day in seven" statute, under which each employee's rest day would be left to one's terms of employment, would result in citizens having different rest days and would not serve the purpose of providing "a day which all members of the family or friends and relatives might spend together."[18] Providing for only "one day's closing per week, at the option of every particular enterpriser," might be, Justice

16 *McGowan v. Maryland*, 366 U.S. 448, 450, 451; 366 U.S. 506, 507, 524 (Frankfurter, J., concurring).

17 *McGowan v. Maryland*, 366 U.S. 520, 438, 507, 504, 478 (Frankfurter, J., concurring).

18 *McGowan v. Maryland*, 366 U.S. 451.

Frankfurter maintained, "disruptive of families whose members are employed by different enterprises."[19] As one member of Parliament argued in the 1936 British parliamentary debates on a proposed Sunday labor law, in a passage cited by both Chief Justice Warren and Justice Frankfurter: "As a family man, let me say that my family life would be unduly disturbed if any member had his Sunday on a Tuesday. The value of a Sunday is that everybody in the family is at home on the same day. What is the use of talking about a six-day working week in which six members of a family would each have his day of rest on a different day of the week?"[20] A common day of rest serves the purpose of providing shared periods of free time not only for family life, the Court argued, but for social and community life more generally. Sunday closing laws provide "a day which all members of the family and community have the opportunity to spend and enjoy together . . . a day on which people may visit friends and relatives who are not available during working days." Citing reports of the International Labour Organization, the justices argued that "the same rest-day should as far as possible be accorded to the members of the same working family and to the working class community as a whole," for such a common day of rest "has an obvious social purpose, namely to enable the workers to take part in the life of the community."[21]

Despite the Supreme Court's ruling in favor of the constitutionality of Sunday labor laws, over the half century since the *McGowan v. Maryland* decision, state legislatures and local governments have widely repealed or otherwise limited their Sunday regulations, often on the basis of liberal principles of religious and economic liberty. At the time of the ruling, more than two-thirds of states had Sunday closing laws. Twenty-five years after the decision, the proportion had dropped to one-third. Since then, that number has diminished still further, and the remaining states with Sunday laws have only further reduced their scope by expanding the lists of exemptions. By 2007, only nine states prohibited, with extensive exemptions, labor and commerce for at least part of Sunday.[22] The trend is the same in Europe. Over the

19 *McGowan v. Maryland*, 366 U.S. 506 (Frankfurter, J., concurring).

20 *McGowan v. Maryland*, 366 U.S. 451 and 366 U.S. 482 (Frankfurter, J., concurring).

21 *McGowan v. Maryland*, 366 U.S. 450, 451.

22 Laband and Heinbuch, *Blue Laws*, 48–49; Lesley Lawrence-Hammer, "Red, White, but Mostly Blue: The Validity of Modern Sunday Closing Laws Under the Establishment Clause," *Vanderbilt Law Review* 60 (2007): 1278.

past two decades in Europe, all countries that have altered their Sunday regulations have moved toward fewer restrictions, and only six countries have maintained restrictive Sunday closing laws.[23]

5.5 A COMMON PERIOD OF FREE TIME

Sunday closing laws face several objections, broadly of two types: first, that they are impermissible; second, that they are infeasible. In the former category, the two leading objections are that Sunday closing laws are incompatible with liberal principles of economic and religious liberty. In the latter category, the two primary objections are, first, that citizens' associational pursuits often depend on the work of others and, second, that some must work be done continuously to meet basic needs. In response, I argue that, if it were properly justified and instituted, the legal protection of a common period of Sunday free time can meet these objections. To distinguish traditional Sunday closing laws from the modified form I suggest, I will refer to the latter as Sunday free time laws. This section aims to establish that Sunday free time laws, again if properly modified, would further effective freedom of association and would be consistent with standard liberal egalitarian principles.

Before turning to the objections and the modifications they require, one distinction to emphasize is that, unlike traditional Sunday closing laws that broadly prohibit Sunday labor and commerce, Sunday free time laws instead guarantee all employees the right to refuse to work on Sundays.[24] Because effective freedom of association requires that citizens have access to shared free

23 Sunday closing laws have become less restrictive in Denmark, Finland, France, Germany, Italy, Portugal, and Spain. Austria, Belgium, Greece, the Netherlands, Norway, and Switzerland have maintained their restrictive laws. Christos Genakos and Svetoslav Danchev, "Evaluating the Impact of Sunday Trading Deregulation" (Centre for Economic Performance Discussion Paper No. 1336, 2015), 15–16.

24 To enforce this right, and following existing laws of this type, employers could be prohibited from soliciting information about this choice during hiring or using refusal as grounds for discharge, discrimination, or any other penalty. To give the protections additional teeth, employers might also be prohibited from giving employees who work Sundays higher compensation or other benefits. For those who are required to be generally available and willing to address work-related matters at any time, particularly managerial and professional employees, the laws might also protect an employee's right to refuse to engage in such work-related tasks on Sundays. These Sunday protections must also be combined with wage and income provisions to ensure that employees can refuse Sunday work without forgoing a decent income.

time, not shared spare time, a prohibition on Sunday labor or commerce is generally not warranted.[25] If, however, the competitive pressures in a given industry or area are so great that an employee's right to refuse to work on Sundays cannot meaningfully be protected, a prohibition on Sunday labor would be justified to ensure effective freedom of association.[26] Prohibitions on Sunday labor are only justified, and to the narrowest extent necessary, if they are the only means to meaningfully guarantee employees the right to not work on Sundays.

The first objection to Sunday closing laws is that they impermissibly conflict with economic liberty, specifically the freedoms to engage in labor or commerce on Sundays. In response to this objection, first, note that even if one takes these economic liberties to have the same status as freedom of association, treating both as basic liberties, this does not entail that economic liberty cannot be regulated to ensure the conditions for the exercise of free association. It is permissible to regulate a basic liberty to protect the exercise of another basic liberty, and protecting employees' right to not work on Sundays—whether with a right of refusal or prohibition if necessary—is such a regulation. Moreover, standard liberal egalitarian principles do *not* hold that these economic liberties are of the same status as freedom of association. Instead, freedom of association is held among the basic liberties, while these economic liberties are not, and the protection of the basic liberties is to have priority over that of the nonbasic liberties.[27] Accordingly, it is permissible to

25 For example, if Smith, assuming she is not sleep deprived, takes a nap on a Sunday afternoon, though she is engaged in personal care (sleeping), that time is still available to devote to her chosen ends, say, if Jones interrupts her nap to invite her to the park. The same is true of paid work beyond what is required to meet one's basic needs, so long as one can freely choose not to engage in the unnecessary work. So, if Smith has the right to refuse to work on Sunday and freely chooses to do so to earn extra money, that time is properly understood as available to devote to her chosen ends, including associating, since she could forgo the Sunday work to engage in other pursuits.

26 J. S. Mill similarly argues, in *On Liberty*, that though Sabbatarian legislation is generally an "illegitimate interference with the rightful liberty of the individual," if the custom of a day of rest "cannot be observed without a general consent to that effect among the industrious classes . . . it may be allowable and right that the law should guarantee to each the observance by others of the custom." Mill, *On Liberty and Other Essays*, ed. John Gray (Oxford: Oxford University Press, 1991), 100.

27 See Samuel Freeman, "Capitalism in the Classical and High Liberal Traditions," *Social Philosophy and Policy* 28 (2011): 19–55; Jeppe von Platz and John Tomasi, "Liberalism and Economic Liberty," in *The Cambridge Companion to Liberalism*, ed. Steven Wall (Cambridge: Cambridge University Press, 2015), 261–81; Alan Patten, "Are the Economic Liberties Basic?" *Critical Review* 26 (2014): 362–74.

regulate the freedom to engage in labor or commerce on Sundays to ensure the conditions for effective freedom of association. If employers cannot hire sufficient numbers of employees who are willing to work on Sundays, the presumable result is that fewer establishments will be open for business on Sundays. This may limit employers' and consumers' ability to engage in market activity, but such a result is permissible because effective freedom of association, as a basic liberty, ought to have priority over the nonbasic economic liberties.

The second objection to Sunday closing laws is that, in providing the resources for the effective exercise of one basic liberty, freedom of association, they impermissibly conflict with another basic liberty, freedom of religion. To meet this objection, Sunday free time laws must be justified and implemented to serve a secular purpose, in two respects: first, in instituting a common period of free time and, second, in specifying that this period be Sunday, rather than a day without any religious connections, as, for instance, Wednesday.[28] The first has been established, as a common period of free time serves the secular purpose of providing the temporal conditions for effective freedom of association. The second, the specification of Sunday, requires additional argument. To be reliable, common period of free time laws must guarantee all employees the right to refuse to work during the common period, and it is preferable if they do so without relying on prohibitions on labor or commerce. Two empirical considerations are then relevant. First, those employees who have nonstandard work schedules are disproportionately those with less education and lower earnings, and as such are less advantaged and have less economic bargaining power.[29] Second, Sunday is a longstanding customary day of rest from labor in the United States, and historical attempts to politically alter the rhythm of the customary week have generally not been successful. For those who have nonstandard work schedules, the right to refuse to work during the common period of free time can be more reliably protected if that period is supported by the weight of custom.[30]

28 Friday is a day of prayer in Islam, Saturday in Judaism. As noted in 5.3, the common period of free time need not be a single, regular day of the week. Wednesday, however, serves as a clear counterproposal to Sunday.

29 Hamermesh, "Changing Inequality in Work Injuries and Work Timing," 23–27.

30 As Justice Frankfurter noted, to attempt to establish a different common day of rest may "prove as futile as the ephemeral decade of the French Republic of 1792." *McGowan v. Maryland*, 366 U.S. 483 (Frankfurter, J., concurring). On the "tremendous resilience of tradition" against political attempts to alter the week, see Zerubavel, *Seven Day Circle*, 27–43, and Witold Rybczynski, *Waiting for the Weekend* (New York: Penguin, 1991), 44–49. If, following

As such, the aim of reliably ensuring the conditions for effective freedom of association provides secular grounds both to establish a common period of free time and to select Sunday as that period.

In addition to serving a secular purpose, Sunday free time laws must also not constrain citizens' religious free exercise, and so ought to include accommodations for those citizens who have a Sabbath day on a different day of the week. These accommodations ought to provide the right to choose, depending on how a particular theory of religious liberty interprets the requirements of free exercise, an alternative or additional day of free time, to be spent in worship, rest, or socialization with co-religionists.[31]

The third objection is that Sunday closing laws are infeasible because citizens' associational pursuits often depend on the work of others. Shared free time laws, generally granting only the right to refuse to work on Sundays rather than prohibiting Sunday labor, go some way toward meeting this objection. But, if guaranteeing the right to refuse to work were to result in fewer businesses being open on Sundays, the objection still arises. That is, the effective freedom of association of some might depend on others working to provide the conditions for that effective freedom.

To consider this objection, take two examples: someone who works in a movie theater and someone who works in transportation. In weighing these conflicts, priority ought to be given to one's effective freedom to pursue a wide range of associational pursuits over one's effective freedom to pursue a narrow range of associational pursuits. In the case of the movie theater employee, her effective freedom to engage in a wide range of associations—any outside of work—ought to have priority over others' narrow interest in associating at the movie theater.[32] In the case of the transportation employee, the priority rule yields a more complex result. Here the conflict is indeed between

---

Justice Sandra Day O'Connor's reasoning in *Lynch v. Donnelly*, 465 U.S. 668, one holds that citizens, particularly those who are non-adherents of a Sunday Sabbath, have an expressive interest in the common period of free time being one without any religious connections, that interest must be weighed against the interest of all citizens, particularly those with the least economic bargaining power, in having reliable access to the common period of free time for effective freedom of association.

31 See Lucas A. Swaine, "Principled Separation: Liberal Governance and Religious Free Exercise," *Journal of Church and State* 38 (1996): 595–619.

32 The value of effective freedom of association and of this priority rule also provides reason to support public spaces, like parks and recreation facilities, in which citizens can engage in a wide range of associational pursuits. Those whose work is required to operate such spaces should then be treated like the transportation employee.

competing claims to engage in a wide range of associational pursuits: the transportation employee's interest in participating in a wide range of associations (any outside of work), and other citizens' interests in participating in a wide range of associations (any that require transportation). In these instances, when the work does provide the conditions for a wide range of associational pursuits, the shifts of Sunday work ought to be done voluntarily or shared on a rotation.[33]

The final objection—that Sunday closing laws are infeasible because some work must be done continuously to meet basic needs, such as emergency services and basic caregiving—indicates that another accommodation of this type is warranted. Those who perform such work as employees ought, like the transportation employee, to do these shifts either voluntarily or on a rotation. Those who provide basic caregiving for their own dependents, as parents or as primary caregivers for the elderly or disabled, ought to have access to public facilities or hired caregiving on Sundays (see 6.4 for further discussion of caregiving). The employees who do this caregiving work should, like other basic needs providing employees, do this work either voluntarily or on a rotation. Caregiving for one's own dependents may, of course, sometimes be done while one is associating with those dependents or with others, and the value of effective freedom of association does provide reason to make those two activities compatible if possible.

Sunday free time laws can meet the objections pressed against traditional Sunday closing laws if they are justified and instituted in these ways: if they are justified on the grounds of reliably providing access to shared free time for effective freedom of association, and if they are instituted to guarantee the right not to work on Sundays (with prohibitions on Sunday work reserved for protecting that right) and with a set of accommodations (for alternative days of religious practice, for work that provides the conditions for a wide range of associational pursuits, and for work that must be done continuously to meet basic needs).

To return to the central claim, social institutions ought to be arranged, insofar as it is possible consistent with the other requirements of justice, such that the temporal coordination problem does not deny citizens effective freedom of association. Sunday free time laws, if they are justified and instituted in these ways, do further effective freedom of association and are consistent

33 As a model, see Walzer's proposal for sharing "dirty work." Walzer, *Spheres of Justice*, 165–83.

with standard liberal egalitarian principles. Beyond this, whether such laws are the best way to arrange social institutions to provide effective freedom of association is an unavoidably circumstantial question. Depending on the relevant circumstances, one or some combination of the other solutions— guaranteeing citizens vast amounts of free time and guaranteeing employees work hours flexibility—or instituting a different common period of free time, may more reliably serve effective freedom of association or may do so with less cost to other appropriately weighted values. If Sunday free time laws are to be opposed, however, it ought to be on these grounds, because there is some more reliable or less costly means of providing for effective freedom of association. As contemporary liberal societies assess whether to maintain, repeal, or reinstitute Sunday closing laws, the laws' function in providing shared free time for effective freedom of association ought to be accorded appropriate weight. More fundamentally, however their claims are realized, citizens ought to be recognized as having legitimate claims to shared free time.

5.6 BEYOND "ALL-PURPOSE MEANS"

The effective freedoms principle is central to liberal egalitarian theories of justice. Different theories of justice realize the effective freedoms principle in different ways, but there is a general tendency to treat both the resources and the liberties monolithically, with reference only to citizens' requirements for "all-purpose means," often solely income and wealth, to exercise their "liberties and opportunities." Yet if the particular resources that are required to exercise particular liberties are never disaggregated and examined separately, these simplifications limit the effective freedoms principle's analytic power and normative reach. For liberal egalitarian principles to realize their full potential, they must be applied with greater attention to the quotidian aspects of citizens' lives, or they will overlook vital problems in social and economic life. One such result of doing so is to recognize something basic, important, yet neglected: that citizens must have shared free time to exercise their freedom of association.

CHAPTER 6

FREE TIME FOR CAREGIVERS

6.1 WORKPLACE ACCOMMODATIONS FOR PARENTS

Among the many Americans who have little free time, working parents are among those with the least, combining significant amounts of paid work with child care obligations, as well as, often, care for their own elderly parents. Women especially experience this time shortage, since women are more likely to be sole providers and caregivers, and women with young children in dual-earner couples still do a greater share of the child care and household labor, working longer total hours.[1]

Given, as I have argued, that all citizens are entitled to a fair share of free time, if—as I will argue it ought to be—parents' basic caregiving is treated as a necessary activity that subtracts from one's free time, like necessary paid work, household labor, personal care, and other forms of caregiving, then parents are in effect entitled to public support. To ensure that parents can have their fair shares of free time while providing this necessary child care, social institutions must be arranged to support parental caregiving.

But beyond this recognition of parental caregiving as a necessary activity, a further question remains: in what form ought this support be provided? Parental support could be provided in such a way that it would allow parents to have free time, while having the choice to do either full-time paid work or full-time caregiving—that is, with public child care provision or income

---

1 Bianchi, "Family Change and Time Allocation in American Families"; Milkie, Raley, and Bianchi, "Taking on the Second Shift."

subsidies for caregivers. Or this public support could come in a form that allows parents to have free time and engage in both paid work and direct caregiving—to have "work-family balance." In addition to income subsidies and public child care provision, public support in this form would include a set of workplace accommodations for parents: periods of paid leave, extended short-hours schedules, and flexible or irregular work hours.

Even if one accepts that caregiving ought to be treated as a necessary activity entitled to public support, are parents (and other caregivers) entitled to such workplace accommodations? A common objection—that parenting should be treated like any other conception of the good—is often pressed against any public support of parenting, but workplace accommodations present a particular challenge for two reasons:

First, in contrast with income subsidies and public provisions, workplace accommodations are more liable to objection because they require more significant changes in existing economic arrangements and they may impose more significant direct costs on other citizens. Workplace accommodations present a strong challenge to the presumption of the "ideal worker"—employees who can work full-time because someone else, a spouse or hired help, fulfills the employee's caregiving obligations—embedded in most employment arrangements. They also may entail that employers and coworkers have to alter their own schedules, perhaps at substantial personal cost, to accommodate parent employees. Second, even if one accepts public support for parents, workplace accommodations require an additional justification to establish that parents are entitled to support in *this* form, rather than only with income subsidies or public child care provision.

One prominent route for defending workplace accommodations on liberal egalitarian grounds is to combine two arguments: a public goods argument and a gender justice argument. First, the public goods argument establishes that parents are entitled to public support because they provide a public good by bearing and rearing children.[2] Second, the gender justice argument establishes that this support ought to be provided in a way that promotes equal

---

2 See, for instance, Linda C. McClain, *The Place of Families: Fostering Capacity, Equality, and Responsibility* (Cambridge, MA: Harvard University Press, 2006), 85–114 and White, *Civic Minimum*, 108–13, 203. Other approaches that rely on a different argument to justify public support for parenting typically still justify workplace accommodations by relying on a supplementary gender justice argument. See, for instance, Maxine Eichner, *The Supportive State: Families, Government, and America's Political Ideals* (Oxford: Oxford University Press, 2010), 75–84.

opportunities for men and women. While I endorse both of these claims, I argue that they are more connected than this two-step approach suggests, and that this disconnect owes to an unduly narrow understanding of what gender justice requires. To justify workplace accommodations, I propose a new way to construct and combine the public goods and gender justice arguments.

I argue that gender justice requires not only that men and women have, as is standardly held, free choice among equal options, but that these choices are made among just background conditions. Specifically, for the conditions with respect to household responsibilities to be just, citizens must be guaranteed their fair shares of free time, with parenting and other forms of basic caregiving treated as necessary activities. Men and women must be able to freely choose from among equal options to (1) engage in paid work and have free time, (2) engage in direct caregiving and have free time, and (3) engage in significant amounts of both paid work and direct caregiving, while having free time.[3] Accordingly, ensuring that men and women can freely choose their household responsibilities from among just conditions requires, in addition to income subsidies and public provisions, workplace accommodations for parents and other caregivers.

6.2 FREE CHOICE AMONG EQUAL OPTIONS

Liberal egalitarian principles entail that unequal outcomes between men and women—specifically, the unequal division of household responsibilities, with women doing a greater share of caregiving—are not necessarily just or unjust.[4] Instead, whether or not such an unequal outcome is just depends on how that result was produced. Liberal egalitarian approaches to gender jus-

---

3 Cf. Nancy Fraser, "After the Family Wage: Gender Equity and the Welfare State," *Political Theory* 22 (1994): 591–618. While Fraser discusses these as alternative models, I argue that citizens ought to have each option.

4 Susan Moller Okin's argument that an equal division of household labor is itself a requirement of liberal egalitarian justice is an exception. Okin argues that justice requires an equal division of household labor because it is necessary to realize equality of opportunity. I follow Richard Arneson in rejecting this claim: a society in which no household had an equal division of labor, but in which households had diverse labor-sharing arrangements, would not necessarily undermine, and indeed would likely foster, equality of opportunity. As such, equality of opportunity does not require equal divisions of household labor. Moreover, contrary to Okin's additional argument for an equal division of household labor—that it is required to teach children a sense of reciprocity—children can learn reciprocity from unequal but fair and diverse household arrangements. Okin, *Justice, Gender, and the Family* (New

tice standardly hold that there are two procedural requirements for an outcome, whether equal or unequal, to be just: (1) it must be the result of men's and women's *free choices*, and (2) men and women must choose from among *equal options*. Furthermore, these conditions must be maintained over time, so that the outcomes that result from free choices among equal options in the present do not undermine free choices among equal options in the future. As such, an unequal division of caregiving labor would be just only if men and women freely chose their household responsibilities from equal options.

Feminists commonly argue that the division of household responsibilities in the contemporary United States is not, in fact, the result of free choices among equal options.[5]

First, they argue, it is unwarranted to regard the choices men and women make as free because, as a result of pervasive gender socialization, they are not necessarily based on genuine preferences. Because children are raised to believe that caregiving and homemaking are primarily women's responsibilities and women's esteem depends more heavily than men's on their qualities as caregivers and homemakers, a woman's choice to do a greater share of household labor should not be regarded as freely made.

Second, men and women do not choose from among equal options because labor market discrimination limits women's option sets. Due to explicit discrimination or implicit bias and statistical discrimination, women are often discriminated against in hiring, promotion, and salary decisions. Accordingly, women have fewer career opportunities and command lower earnings than men. When more women than men choose to forgo paid work in favor of household labor, those choices were not made from among equal options.[6]

Third, they argue, men and women do not have equal options because the all-things-considered costs of their choices are unequal. For the same choice to pursue a successful career, men and women face different material, psychological, and social burdens. In the same occupational position, women are more likely than men to have greater difficulty fulfilling caregiving expectations

York: Basic Books, 1989); Arneson, "Feminism and Family Justice," *Public Affairs Quarterly* 11 (1997): 313–30.

5 See Anca Gheaus, "Gender Justice," *Journal of Ethics and Social Philosophy* 6 (2012): 1–24, and Kristi A. Olson, "Our Choices, Our Wage Gap?," *Philosophical Topics* 40 (2012): 47–48.

6 For the argument that the ideal worker model itself discriminates against women because it is based on a "masculine norm," see Joan Williams, *Unbending Gender: Why Work and Family Conflict and What to Do about It* (Oxford: Oxford University Press, 2000).

and obligations, have a greater risk of exposure to sexual harassment, have greater difficulty finding a compatible romantic partner, and must expend greater effort navigating and counteracting stereotypes. Again, if women choose to do a greater share of household labor than men, that choice was not made from among equal options.

There is ample evidence of each of these constraints on women's choices. It is easier, however, to accept the negative case—that existing gender dynamics make choices unfree and options unequal—than it is to construct the positive case—identifying the particular conditions that must obtain for choices to be free and options equal. It is both empirically difficult to know to what extent the present unequal division of household responsibilities is the result of unfree choices among unequal options, and theoretically difficult to specify what conditions would have to obtain for an unequal division to be entirely the result of free choices from among equal options.[7]

Difficult does not, of course, mean impossible, and there are compelling accounts of what free choice among equal options requires. Yet, even if one accepted one of these accounts of the conditions of free choice and equal options, it would not constitute a full account of what gender justice requires. Even if the conditions were met, such that men and women freely chose their household responsibilities from among equal options, if an unequal outcome results, such that women do a greater share of household labor, there may still be a gender injustice. As I argue in the following section, liberal egalitarian gender justice requires not only that men and women freely choose their household responsibilities from among equal options, but also that their choices must be from among just background conditions.[8]

---

7 As one economic study notes, "There is considerable evidence to support the belief that gender differences in preferences play some role in gender differences in occupations. The claim that discrimination is also important is more controversial. It is not an easy matter to distinguish between the two empirically." Francine D. Blau and Lawrence M. Kahn, "Gender Differences in Pay," *Journal of Economic Perspectives* 14 (2000): 88–89. For an argument that these complexities can be sidestepped by taking an unequal outcome in the division of labor between men and women as evidence of unequal options or opportunities, see Anne Phillips, "Defending Equality of Outcome," *Journal of Political Philosophy* 12 (2004): 1–19.

8 My argument is indebted to Olson's "Our Choices, Our Wage Gap?" Olson argues that the gender wage gap is still objectionable—even if it is the result of men and women's freely made choices, reflecting their genuine preferences, among equal options—if the options themselves are unfair.

6.3 FREE CHOICE AMONG JUST BACKGROUND CONDITIONS

Within liberal egalitarian theories of justice, the normative significance of free choice is twofold. First, it is valuable to the individual citizen, in that it allows one's choices to realize and reflect one's conception of the good. Second, it plays a legitimating role, in that it allows citizens to be held responsible for the consequences of their choices. But, to have this value and this legitimating function, citizens' free choices must occur among just background conditions.

Suppose that all citizens have equal occupational option sets: being a miner in a toxic environment, a gardener for below subsistence wages, or a waiter exposed to regular harassment. Suppose also that each of these conditions— working in a toxic environment, for below subsistence wages, or exposed to harassment—is unjust. If one chooses to be a gardener, miner, or waiter, that choice does not reliably realize or reflect one's conception of the good, nor does it render one without legitimate grounds for complaint if one is sick, poor, or harassed.

The required just background conditions—if free choice is to have its full normative significance—are, for any given choice, what justice requires generally in that domain. Suppose justice requires that one be permitted to marry or not marry, and to marry someone of the opposite sex or the same sex, but that the law prohibits same-sex marriage. If one has the choice only to marry no one or someone of the opposite sex, the conditions of one's choice are not just. If someone then chooses to not marry, this cannot be taken to reflect her conception of the good or render her without legitimate basis for complaint about any resulting deficiencies she suffers. In order for just background conditions to obtain, one's option set must include all of the conditions required by justice.[9]

Free choice among just background conditions is integral to liberal egalitarian theories of justice. The requirements this principle imposes for free choice to be fully valuable and legitimating apply to citizens, as such, across all domains in which choice is normatively significant. The principle could be articulated and applied without any reference to gender (or any other identity characteristic of citizens). Indeed, in the perfectly just society, there

---

9 In this respect, the conditions for fully valuable and legitimating free choice are more demanding than those for voluntary choice, which is generally taken to require that one have more than one acceptable choice. See Serena Olsaretti, *Liberty, Desert, and the Market: A Philosophical Study* (Cambridge: Cambridge University Press, 2004), 137–61.

would be no reason to specify that *men and women* ought to have free choice among just background conditions.

It is, however, valuable to specify the principle with respect to gender for two reasons: First, given the depth and pervasiveness of gender injustice, and the long and ongoing political and intellectual disputes about what gender justice requires, it is important to determine and articulate how liberal egalitarian principles apply to gender. Second, given that existing societies are not perfectly just, developing the principle with respect to gender allows for assessments of whether existing unequal outcomes between men and women are unobjectionable or instances of gender injustice.

When applied to gender, liberal egalitarian principles require not only that men and women have free choice among equal options, but also that they choose from among just background conditions. Just background conditions encompass the requirements for equal options *and* extend to the requirements for substantive conditions in a given domain. The conditions under which men and women, or citizens generally, choose may be unjust without being unequal.[10] An unequal division of household responsibilities, with women doing a greater share of caregiving labor, is unjust, even if household responsibilities are freely chosen from among equal options, if they are chosen from among unjust background conditions.

It is at this point that free time enters centrally into the discussion. With respect to one's choice of household responsibilities, one condition of particular importance must obtain: all citizens must have their fair shares of free time, with caregiving for children and other dependents treated as necessary activities. This condition, as an extension of free time's general neglect, has not been widely recognized. Indeed, this inattention to free time may be part of the explanation for why the requirement for just background conditions, as a condition apart from free choice and equal options, has not been given much, if any, attention in liberal theories of gender justice.

The requirement that citizens be guaranteed their fair shares of free time, with caregiving for children and other dependents treated as necessary activities, entails that citizens must freely choose their household responsibilities from among the options to (1) engage in paid work and have free time,

---

10 The principle of free choice among just background conditions is suggested by Rawls when he argues that a traditionally gendered division of household responsibilities is not unjust only if "it is fully voluntary and does not result from or lead to injustice." Rawls, "Idea of Public Reason Revisited," 161. Rawls, however, focuses in his brief discussion of the gendered division of labor on the conditions of voluntariness and equality.

(2) engage in direct caregiving and have free time, and (3) engage in significant amounts of both paid work and caregiving, while still having free time. Ensuring that citizens have the third option requires workplace accommodations for parents and other caregivers.

6.4 JUST BACKGROUND CONDITIONS FOR HOUSEHOLD RESPONSIBILITIES

Suppose that men and women, specifically parents, do have free choice among equal options, and that these options are (1) to do sixty hours of paid work per week, with a partner who does sixty hours of direct caregiving; (2) to do sixty hours of direct caregiving with a partner who does sixty hours of paid work; and (3) to do forty hours of paid work and thirty hours of direct caregiving, with a partner who does the same. When freely choosing among these equal options, suppose that most men choose (1) and most women choose (2) or (3). As a result, household responsibilities are divided unequally between men and women, with women doing a greater share of caregiving.

Even though men and women have free choice among equal options, the conditions of those options are unjust. The options must provide one with one's fair share of free time, with basic caregiving for children and other dependents treated as a necessary activity.

The argument for the first half—that citizens are entitled to a fair share of free time—is the argument of Chapters 3 and 4: that citizens are entitled to a fair share of the resource of free time on the basis of the effective freedoms principle. The argument for the second half—that basic caregiving for children ought to be treated as a necessary activity—remains to be presented here.

Recall from 3.8 that, on any liberal egalitarian theory of justice, society has a general obligation to ensure, insofar as doing so is consistent with the other requirements of justice, that the basic needs of those who are unable or cannot reasonably be expected to meet them are met. This general obligation entails that, in addition to the necessary activities one must do to meet one's own basic needs, there is another set of necessary activities that society generally must do to meet the basic needs of those who are unable to do so themselves.

When one does unpaid basic caregiving for one's spouse, parent, or other close relation, one is partially discharging this general obligation of society.

One is doing the necessary activities that must be done to ensure that the basic needs of those who are unable to meet them are met. As such, this basic caregiving ought to be recognized as a necessary activity that subtracts from one's share of free time (rather than as a use of one's free time). This caregiving is objectively necessary to meet a basic need; the basic need is just, in this case, of someone other than oneself. To treat unpaid basic caregiving as a necessary activity is in effect to make such caregiving eligible for public support, so that one can do this caregiving and have free time.

One might accept the foregoing argument with respect to caregiving for adults who are disabled, ill, or infirm, but reject it for caregiving for children. Child care is different, it is argued, in that procreative parents do not simply discharge a general obligation to meet the basic needs of those who are unable to do so; rather, they create a new obligation, that is, the care of a person who would otherwise not have existed. Like all citizens, parents ought to bear the costs of their choices, and so ought to be required to use their own resource shares to meet the basic needs of their children. It would be unfair for other citizens, the argument goes, particularly those who choose not to have children, to be required to give up some of their resource shares to publicly support child care.[11] Children, to push this argument to its rhetorical limit, are personal projects like any other, and parents have no more claim to additional public support to pursue their particular conceptions of the good than do any other citizens.

Some dismiss this argument outright: however children are created, once they exist, they are members of society, and society has a general obligation to ensure their basic needs are met. Those who take this or similar views readily accept that basic child care, like other forms of caregiving, ought to be regarded as a necessary activity. Yet, even if one is sympathetic to this responsibility argument—as others are—it can be overcome by establishing that parents produce public goods by creating and raising children. Children provide a range of nonexcludable benefits to society, and so parents, as producers of a public good, are entitled to public support and basic child care ought to be treated as a necessary activity.[12] I here state and endorse what I

11 See, for example, Rakowski, *Equal Justice*, 153.

12 The most prominent proponents of this argument are Nancy Folbre and Rolf George. See Folbre, "Children as Public Goods?," *American Economic Review* 84 (1994): 86–90; Folbre, *The Invisible Heart: Economics and Family Values* (New York: New Press, 2001); Folbre, *Valuing Children: Rethinking the Economics of the Family* (Cambridge, MA: Harvard University Press, 2008); George, "Who Should Bear the Cost of Children?," *Public Affairs Quarterly* 1 (1987):

take to be the best version of this argument, with my addition only to show how it entails that parental caregiving ought to be treated as a necessary activity that subtracts from one's free time.

There are two versions of the public goods argument, one from economic efficiency and one from fairness.[13] Public goods are nonrivalrous, in that one person's consumption of the good does not reduce another's, and nonexcludable, in that it is either impossible or too costly to exclude noncontributors from enjoyment of the good. The economic efficiency argument holds that, if there is a risk of the public good being undersupplied, because it is costly to produce and the benefits are nonexcludable, it is justified for the state to intervene to incentivize the production of the good. The fairness argument holds even if there is no risk that the good will be undersupplied. Instead, the principle of fairness holds that whenever some people bear costs to produce a benefit as part of a cooperative scheme, it is unfair for others in that cooperative scheme to free ride on their efforts. All beneficiaries have an enforceable obligation to do their fair share to maintain the cooperative scheme, or to bear a fair share of the costs.[14]

It is the fairness argument that supports parents' claim to public support of child care, and it is the nonexcludability of the benefits of children that is of particular importance to this argument. By creating and raising children, parents produce three significant nonexcludable benefits.[15]

First, the creation and raising of children ensures that society will continue with another generation. For a wide range of conceptions of the good, the meaning of one's projects and achievements depends in part on the existence of future generations to recognize and appreciate what one has accomplished and to sustain and continue what one has done.[16] All those whose conceptions

---

1–42; George, "On the External Benefits of Children," in *Kindred Matters: Rethinking the Philosophy of the Family*, ed. Diana Tietjens Meyers, Kenneth Kipnis, and Cornelius F. Murphy, Jr. (Ithaca: Cornell University Press, 1993).

13 Paula Casal and Andrew Williams, "Rights, Equality and Procreation," *Analyse & Kritik* 17 (1995): 103–4.

14 Serena Olsaretti, "Children as Public Goods?," *Philosophy & Public Affairs* 41 (2013): 232–38. For prominent statements of the principle of fairness, or fair play, see Hart, "Are There Any Natural Rights?," *Philosophical Review* 64 (1955): 175–91; Rawls, *Theory of Justice*, orig. ed., 108–14; and Klosko, *Political Obligations* (Oxford: Oxford University Press, 2005).

15 White, *Civic Minimum*, 110–11.

16 See Samuel Scheffler, *Death and the Afterlife*, Niko Kolodny ed. (Oxford: Oxford University Press, 2013).

of the good depend in part on this intergenerational continuance, including those who do not have children, benefit from the creation and rearing of a succeeding generation, and it is impossible to be excluded from this benefit.

Second, and more concretely, children are the future tax base whose contributions will fund public expenditures. When the present generation has retired from economic productivity, the maintenance of society will depend on the tax contributions of this next generation. This benefit is most plain in a pay-as-you-go welfare state, in which the retirement benefits of the older generation are funded by the taxes of the younger working generation. It is technically possible to exclude nonparents from these welfare benefits, by establishing two separate welfare systems, one funded by and for parents and one by and for nonparents, but such a divided welfare scheme is inconsistent with a core tenet of liberal egalitarian justice, that society is a joint endeavor in which all citizens share in one another's fates.[17]

Third, and most decisively, members of the present generation will depend on the labor of a succeeding generation to support them as they age. When members of the present generation are no longer productive and become infirm, they will require a younger generation to produce the goods to sustain them and provide their care. It is impossible, or at least deeply inconsistent with basic principles of morality, for nonparents to be excluded from this future benefit of children, for to do so would be to ensure their demise at the point at which they could no longer be supported by members of their own generation.[18]

The creation and rearing of children is, as such, a public good in the relevant respect, in that children, as future adults, provide nonexcludable benefits to both parents and nonparents. Parents alone incur costs to produce a good that benefits all citizens. Moreover, in doing so, they intentionally participate in a benefits-producing cooperative scheme, namely, the maintenance of society and generations over time, as they create and raise functioning and productive members of society.[19] As such, the principle of fairness applies: because par-

---

17 Olsaretti argues that children should be recognized as "socialized goods," rather than public goods, because though this benefit can be excluded, we intentionally structure our institutions so that it cannot. Children are, however, still nonexcludable public goods with respect to the first and third benefits. Olsaretti, "Children as Public Goods?," 248–58.

18 As Elizabeth Anderson notes, "As long as one doesn't plan to commit suicide once the next generation enters the workforce, one can't help but demand the labor services of future generations." Anderson, "What Is the Point of Equality?," 324.

19 Olsaretti, "Children as Public Goods?," 239–47.

enting is a cost-incurring, benefit-producing activity in a cooperative scheme, it is wrong for nonparents to free ride on their labor. The beneficiaries of parents' caregiving labor, all citizens, have an obligation to do their fair share to maintain, or to fairly share the costs, of their cooperative activity, that is, by publicly supporting caregiving.[20]

Caregiving for children ought, then, to be treated as other forms of caregiving for the ill, disabled, and infirm. Though procreative parents are responsible for creating a new obligation (the satisfaction of the child's basic needs), they alone are not responsible for meeting that obligation. There is a general obligation to ensure that children's basic needs are met, and all members of society are required to do their fair share, or to fairly share in the costs, to do so.[21] In this way, caregiving for children is not different from caregiving for adult dependents. Because caregiving for each is an objectively necessary activity to meet a basic need, it is appropriately recognized as a necessary activity that subtracts from one's free time. When parental basic caregiving is treated as a necessary activity, it is in effect to make such caregiving eligible for public support, so that parents can do this caregiving and have free time.

Liberal egalitarian principles of justice require, then, that citizens are guaranteed a fair share of free time, with basic caregiving for children and other dependents treated as necessary activities. In the final section, I show how the requirement that this just background condition obtains justifies workplace accommodations for parents.

20 This argument warrants two important clarifications. First, if a given child is not expected to provide the three benefits as an adult, e.g., due to severe disability, I here assume that the child's parenting still ought to be publicly supported, because to do otherwise would be contrary to other important values, including social equality and reproductive choice. Second, once a generation is of a certain size, additional children may not provide any further benefits and may produce countervailing costs. (And, as technology develops and environmental constraints increase, this beneficial population level may diminish.) The recognition of procreative parents' basic child care as a necessary activity must, in a way that is consistent with other liberal egalitarian values, take this into account. As additional children above some rate of population growth no longer provide public goods, the ideal policy would, for parents' additional children beyond this point, treat a proportionally greater amount of the parents' caregiving as a use of their free time. Any such policy must be targeted to diminishing public support for parents' free time, without diminishing essential support for children's well-being. For a similar treatment of parenting labor, see White, *Civic Minimum*, 111.

21 Beyond the general social obligation to ensure that children's basic needs are met, parents may have additional special obligations to their children, and so may be morally obligated to provide nonbasic caregiving to their children in their free time.

6.5 WORK-FAMILY BALANCE

When citizens choose their divisions of household responsibilities, those divisions must be freely chosen from among just background conditions, conditions that include the requirements for both equal options and substantive justice in that domain. With respect to household responsibilities, a substantive requirement of justice of particular importance is that citizens must be guaranteed their fair shares of free time, with basic caregiving for children and other dependents treated as necessary activities that subtract from free time. This requirement for just background conditions entails that citizens can freely choose from among three options.

First, citizens, including parents and those with other caregiving responsibilities, must have the options to (1) engage in full-time paid work while having free time, and (2) engage in full-time direct caregiving while having free time. (By direct caregiving, I mean labor that itself meets a child's basic needs, e.g., feeding, bathing, monitoring, to be distinguished from indirect caregiving, e.g., labor to earn an income to purchase or hire the satisfaction of the child's basic needs.)[22] Ensuring these options requires that those engaged in full-time caregiving be eligible for income subsidies (so they can do unpaid caregiving and meet their own and their dependents' basic needs) and that those engaged in full-time paid work be eligible for subsidized or publicly provided child care (so they can do paid work and still meet their dependents' basic needs). The condition that citizens must be guaranteed free time entails these two options because they are necessary to ensure that citizens have free time within, consistent with freedom of occupational choice, their chosen occupation. Because parental caregiving provides a public good and fulfills society's general obligation to ensure that the basic needs of those who are unable to meet them are met, and is as such a necessary activity, it ought to be recognized as a legitimate occupational category.

In addition to these two options, citizens must also have the option (3) to engage in significant amounts of both paid work and direct caregiving, while having free time. It is to ensure this option that workplace accommodations for parents are required, as adjusted work schedules allow parents to engage in both paid work and direct caregiving.

---

22 Both are appropriately regarded as necessary activities, a feature that is taken into account in these options.

The justification for this third option depends on the conjunction of the previous conditions—that citizens are entitled to free time, with caregiving recognized as a necessary activity, in their chosen occupation—with another: that providers of public goods are entitled to public support in a form that allows them to realize their legitimate interests in providing the public good. The principle of fairness does not require that providers of a public good have solely altruistic motives, only that they intentionally participate in a cooperative benefits-producing scheme, and so they may have their own legitimate interests to realize in providing the good.[23] Parents have a legitimate interest in having a continuing and close parent-child relationship, as this relationship provides unique goods through its particular combination of fiduciary responsibilities and intimacy.[24] While it is possible for parents to have such a relationship without engaging in direct caregiving, to be unable to engage in such direct caregiving does limit their opportunity to have this relationship.[25] Given that parents have legitimate interests in raising children and that they are entitled to public support as producers of a public good, it would be unfair to give them this support in a form that does not provide them the opportunity to realize their interests in having children.

If parents have only option (1), to engage in full-time paid work and have free time, they cannot engage in substantial direct caregiving (for, recall, direct caregiving is labor that itself meets a child's basic needs and is a necessary activity that subtracts from one's free time). If parents have only options (1) and (2), to engage in either full-time paid work or full-time direct caregiving and have free time, they cannot exercise their freedom of occupational

23 Olsaretti, "Children as Public Goods?," 246–47.

24 Harry Brighouse and Adam Swift, "Parents' Rights and the Value of the Family," *Ethics* 117 (2006): 91–101. As Rob Reich puts it, "Raising a child is never merely a service rendered unto another person but is the collective sharing of a life. . . . Adults often have children in order to fulfill their goal to have a family and to live life as part of a family," and have a "self-regarding interest" in a "close and abiding relationship" with their children. Reich, *Bridging Liberalism and Multiculturalism in American Education* (Chicago: University of Chicago Press, 2002), 149.

25 As Brighouse and Swift note, "The conscientious parent, living in poverty, doing her best to provide her child with a decent start in life, may find herself working longer hours, or trying to hold down two or more jobs, in a way that makes it very difficult for her to enjoy an intimate relationship with them. . . . [Furthermore,] jobs, especially in the United States, frequently lack the kind of employment protection that enables parents to negotiate their hours of work to fit with the demands of parenting, and jobs are often structured in such a way that wholehearted involvement in them is strongly in tension with wholehearted involvement in family life." Brighouse and Swift, "Parents' Rights and the Value of the Family," 106–8.

choice, have free time, and engage in direct caregiving (for the first reason, with the addition that the occupational choice that provides these conditions would be limited to one).

Instead, they must, in addition to options (1) and (2), have option (3), to engage in significant amounts of both paid work and direct caregiving, while having free time. This option ensures that they can have free time, within their chosen occupation, and engage in direct caregiving. Providing this option requires a set of workplace accommodations for parents, including periods of paid leave, extended short-hours schedules, and flexible work hours.

6.6 GENDER JUSTICE

Gender justice requires not only that men and women have free choice among equal options, but that their choices are made within the context of just background conditions. With respect to household responsibilities, men and women may have free choice among equal options, but those options might themselves be unjust. It is unjust, as I have argued, if men and women must choose from among options that do not allow them to engage in paid work, direct caregiving, or both, while having free time and working in their chosen occupation. Ensuring these options requires that parents have access to income subsidies for direct caregiving, subsidized or publicly provided child care, and workplace accommodations.

Many men and women, if not most, in the contemporary United States do not have these options. Household responsibilities are also unequally divided between men and women, with women doing a greater share of caregiving labor. This is unjust, twice over. It is unjust, without any reference to gender, if citizens are not guaranteed their fair shares of free time. In addition to this temporal or economic injustice, it is a gender injustice if an unequal outcome between men and women results from their choices among unjust conditions. To find the unequal division of household responsibilities between men and women objectionable, it is not necessary to know whether their choices were unfree or their options unequal; it is sufficient to know that their options were themselves unjust.

CHAPTER 7

CONCLUSION

Time for What We Will

7.1 PROVIDING FREE TIME

In the just society, all citizens would be guaranteed their fair shares of free time, time they could devote at their discretion to their own ends. But to how much free time are citizens entitled? And how are citizens' claims to free time to be guaranteed? This final chapter addresses these two questions. Answering the question of "how much" requires, among other considerations, weighing the value of additional time against additional money. Answering the question of "how" depends on identifying the essential features of citizens' claims and possible ways of realizing them.

Addressing these questions reveals two additional and significant implications. First, recognizing citizens' claims to free time provides grounds to bolster and adjudicate a range of contested welfare and employment policies. Liberal theories of justice have justified labor and employment regulations on an array of contingent grounds, producing overlapping and at times conflicting justifications. The claim to free time provides foundational grounds to justify a diverse set of policies, as well as a principle that can both settle existing policy disputes and yield new and unorthodox policy ideas.

Second, recognizing free time as a resource that is valuable to citizens in the same way as the resources of income and wealth provides grounds to challenge the presumption in favor of unceasing economic growth as a social goal. Once a society has reached a certain degree of development, additional temporal resources may be of greater value to citizens' effective freedom than additional material resources, and so a society may justly choose to forgo more material wealth in favor of more free time.

7.2 HOW MUCH? DETERMINING FAIR SHARES

In reply to the claim that all citizens are entitled to a fair share of free time, a sensible practical question is, to how much free time are citizens entitled? Because the argument applies across a range of theories and to different societies, and given the attendant variation in how the relevant principles might be applied and in empirical circumstances, there is no single answer to provide. It is, however, possible to provide an explanation of how to determine an answer, by describing the considerations relevant to what constitutes a fair share. In a wealthy society, as this will show, the answer is likely at least the "eight hours for what we will" demanded by early labor reformers, if not more. Yet, whatever the prescribed amount, and whether this amounts to more or less than citizens in existing societies have on average, the important point is that in the just society *all* citizens would have their fair share of free time, and they would have that free time *by right*.

To determine what constitutes a fair share of free time, there are four relevant considerations:

(1) how much time a society must devote to the shared burdens of social cooperation

(2) which distributive principles apply to citizens' resource claims

(3) the relative weights given to different resources

(4) whether any special intervening reasons apply to an individual's claim

The first consideration depends on how demanding the shared burdens of social cooperation are, according to the background theory of justice, and how much time is required to meet those shared burdens. Consistent with standard liberal egalitarian principles, I have assumed that society has a general obligation to ensure, insofar as is possible consistent with the other requirements of justice, that the basic needs of all its members are met (see 3.8). Meeting this general social obligation, or any further shared burdens, requires some amount of time-consuming labor.[1] How much time depends on empirical circumstances, particularly a society's level of material wealth and technological development. Though the levels of functioning associated with the basic needs vary across societies (see 3.7), generally, the more technologically advanced and wealthier a society is, the less time a society must expend to meet the basic needs of all its members. These two factors—how demanding a society's shared burdens are and how much time is required to meet them—determine the aggregate amount of free time available in a society. Thus, in two societies with the same obligation to meet the basic needs of their members and assuming no obligations across the two societies, there may be little aggregate free time available in an impoverished and less technological developed society and an abundance of aggregate free time available in a wealthy and technologically developed society.

From this aggregate available amount of free time, the next consideration is which distributive principle applies to citizens' resource claims, that is whether an egalitarian, sufficientarian, prioritarian, or other principle. Which principle applies depends on the particular theory of justice, and as discussed in 4.5, the relevant principle for citizens' claims to free time may differ from that applied to citizens' other resource claims. Before addressing the third consideration—the relative weights given to different resources—at greater length, the final consideration is whether any special intervening reasons apply to an individual's claim. The primary reasons of this type, as discussed in 4.7, relate to an individual's choice of occupation. If someone, given the first three considerations, would have a claim to eight hours of free time per day, but chose an occupation, such as being self-employed or in the military, to the effect that her pro tanto claim to free time in her chosen occupation is overridden by an intervening reason, she may be entitled to less than would otherwise be her fair share.

The third consideration—how citizens' claims to free time are weighted against their claims to other resources—warrants greater attention, both for its greater complexity and for an implication it raises about the value of economic growth. Citizens are entitled to free time on the basis of the effective freedoms principle, which holds that citizens are entitled to a fair share of the resources that are generally required to exercise their formal liberties and

---

1 See Stanczyk, "Productive Justice."

opportunities. But free time is not the only resource to which the principle applies; citizens also generally require the resources of income and wealth (among others). Thus, on the basis of the effective freedoms principle, citizens are entitled to a fair share of a bundle of resources—both temporal and material—to exercise their freedoms. Because both resources are generally required and because money is imperfectly substitutable for time (see 4.4), this bundle must include some amount of both resources. This raises the question of how citizens' bundles ought to be allocated between the resources of free time and the resources of income and wealth, a question that is complicated by the fact that the relationship between the two resources is dynamic. There is a trade-off, both at a given time and over time, between being able to guarantee more free time or more income and wealth.

The trade-off is most readily apparent between income and leisure, understood as time not engaged in paid work. As the neoclassical economic model of labor supply depicts, at any given time, there is an inverse relationship between income and leisure, as individuals choose between engaging in income-earning work or income-forgoing leisure. And, over time, if productivity increases, those gains from productivity can either be taken in the form of fewer work hours and more leisure or constant work hours and more production.[2] The trade-off between leisure and income is not necessarily constant, since under some circumstances more leisure time may increase labor productivity or labor force participation, but there is still, under any set of circumstances, a trade-off at some point between more leisure and more production, and thus more income and wealth.

A similar, though less pronounced, trade-off exists between income and free time. The trade-off arises for two reasons: first, because guaranteeing free time requires wealth-consuming public provisions and targeted subsidies (as I will discuss in 7.3) and, second, because citizens may choose to spend their guaranteed free time not engaging in income-earning work or economic production. Thus, guaranteeing greater amounts of free time may constrain economic production and, in turn, the amount of income and wealth available to citizens, such that to guarantee citizens a greater amount of free time may limit the amount of income and wealth that citizens can be guaranteed.

---

2 On the conflict between economic growth and leisure time under capitalism, see G. A. Cohen, *Karl Marx's Theory of History: A Defence*, expanded ed. (1978; repr., Princeton: Princeton University Press, 2000), 296–325 and Van Parijs, *Real Freedom for All*, 186–233.

To be clear, though a trade-off between greater free time and greater income and wealth may, in many circumstances, be likely to occur, its existence or magnitude is not a certainty. Some of the reasons the trade-off might be moderated are the same as those that would apply to guaranteed leisure: depending on labor market dynamics, guaranteeing citizens a greater amount of free time may increase productivity (if workers are more productive working shorter shifts) and increase labor force participation (if caregivers and the disabled take advantage of shorter work shifts to enter the labor force).[3] But there is also an important way in which the relationship between income and free time is different from that between income and leisure: that is, one can choose to spend one's guaranteed free time engaged in paid work or economic production. Someone who presently works long hours, if guaranteed the opportunity to work shorter hours, may choose not to take advantage of that opportunity and instead to continue working long hours. Or someone might work shorter hours in her current employment and use the newly available free time to moonlight or begin a new business venture. Thus, though providing citizens with a greater amount of free time would, at some point, almost certainly reduce a society's level of economic growth and possible material wealth, the existence and extent of this trade-off may vary.

Given, then, that citizens' bundles must include some amount of both resources, and assuming there is a trade-off between guaranteeing more free time and more income and wealth, how should the bundles be allocated across resources? More pointedly, how much free time should citizens be guaranteed, in light of the fact that, at some point, guaranteeing greater shares of free time is likely to come at the cost of diminished economic production and smaller shares of income and wealth?

Though the trade-off between time and money has been neglected, in its general form, this problem is not a new one for theories of justice, for it arises whenever citizens have dynamic multidimensional claims. An example is the potential conflict between Rawls's primary goods of income and wealth and the powers and prerogatives of office. If the powers and prerogatives of office are realized through workplace democracy and broad citizen control over the means of production, guaranteeing citizens a greater share of this resource

---

3 Francine D. Blau and Lawrence M. Kahn, "Female Labor Supply: Why Is the United States Falling Behind?," *American Economic Review* 103 (2013): 251–56.

may reduce the society's total economic production, and so reduce citizens' shares of income and wealth.[4]

This difficulty is handled on Rawls's theory of justice, as, in some form, on most liberal egalitarian theories, by the construction of an index, which bundles and assigns relative weights and marginal values to the different primary goods. If one resource is of lesser relative value or of more diminishing marginal value, sacrifices in it ought to be made for the sake of greater shares of the more valuable resources. Specifying such an index in any detail is, of course, a complex task, and thus most theories only suggest how an index would be constructed.

There are three general approaches that might be taken. To be clear, whichever approach is followed, citizens must be guaranteed some amount of free time on the grounds of the effective freedoms principle. Beyond this, first, the relative weights may be empirically determined. If, for instance, a theory holds that justice requires maximizing the real freedom of the least advantaged position, the theory could hold that, in any given circumstances, a specific ratio of free time to income and wealth would in fact maximize the least advantaged's real freedom. Second, the index might be constructed by relying on intuitive judgments of what would be rationally prudent for the least advantaged. This is the approach Rawls explicitly endorses: "weighting primary goods" is done "by taking up the standpoint of the representative individual from this group and asking which combination of primary social goods it would be rational for him to prefer."[5] On these two approaches, the relative value of time to money could be determined, based on either empirical facts or hypothetical or intuitive judgments, without reference to the judgments of the society's members.

On the third approach, the relative weights of the resources in the index would be determined democratically, as a society could popularly decide whether to guarantee a greater share of or aim to maximize one resource over another.[6] A society might democratically choose to guarantee a greater

4 For a discussion of this conflict, see Freeman, *Rawls*, 112–15, 133–34; Freeman, "Capitalism in the Classical and High Liberal Traditions," 47–52; and Samuel Arnold, "Work as It Might Be: A Theory of Justice in Production" (PhD diss., Princeton University, 2011), 179–81.

5 Rawls, *Theory of Justice*, rev. ed., 80.

6 The second and third approaches might converge if the determination ought to be made democratically by citizens deliberating from the perspective of what it would be rational for the representative least advantaged individual to prefer.

amount of free time and accept lower rates of economic growth and shares of income and wealth, or it might choose the opposite.[7] Rawls, in fact, describes such a choice, suggesting this approach: two societies may have justly unequal levels of wealth if, he contends, "the first decides to industrialize and to increase its rate of (real) saving, while the second does not. Being content with things as they are, and preferring a more pastoral and leisurely society, the second reaffirms its social values. Some decades later the first country is twice as wealthy as the second."[8]

The question of how to weight time relative to money has implications for the value of economic growth. Consider the following puzzle. Rawls consistently maintains, without argument, that a just society could have a rate of zero economic growth, like J. S. Mill's "just stationary state."[9] Yet, Rawls also holds that justice requires that society's economic institutions work to maximize the position of the least advantaged over time. If economic growth would improve the conditions of the least advantaged, there appears to be a contradiction in the claim that a just society could cease economic growth.

The leading account of how to reconcile this apparent tension, offered by Samuel Freeman, is drawn from Rawls's contention that, rather than "great wealth," "what men want is meaningful work in free association with others."[10] The position of the least advantaged is measured with an index that includes the powers and prerogatives of office and the social bases of self-respect in addition to income and wealth. Compared to the institutions of capitalist ownership and employment, the institutions of collective ownership and workplace democracy may provide the least advantaged with smaller shares of income and wealth, but greater shares of the powers and prerogatives of office and the social bases of self-respect. Depending on how the primary goods are weighted in the index, the institutions of workplace democracy may be more to the benefit of the least advantaged than the institutions of

---

7 Bertrand Russell suggests this approach, recommending a "popular vote to decide," at regular intervals, "whether more leisure or more goods were to be preferred." Russell, "In Praise of Idleness," in *In Praise of Idleness: And Other Essays*, (1935; repr., Abingdon: Routledge, 2004), 10.

8 Rawls, *Law of Peoples*, 117.

9 Ibid., 107; Rawls, *Justice as Fairness*, 67, 159; J. S. Mill, *Principles of Political Principles of Political Economy and Chapters on Socialism*, ed. Jonathan Riley (Oxford: Oxford University Press, 1994), 124–30.

10 Rawls, *Theory of Justice*, rev. ed., 257–58. This account is offered by Freeman in *Rawls*, 111–14, 133–34 and "Capitalism in the Classical and High Liberal Traditions," 47–52.

capitalist employment, and accordingly more compatible with justice. Furthermore, it is possible that the institutions of workplace democracy could result in the cessation of economic growth and still be to the greatest benefit to the least advantaged.

This reconstruction of Rawls's argument has been met with skepticism that a plausible index would weigh the powers and prerogatives of office and the social bases of self-respect, specifically as realized by workplace democracy, such that it could be to the benefit to the least advantaged to forgo any gains in income and wealth. Such an index, according to this objection, gives both too much weight to the position and status goods provided by workplace democracy and too little weight to further gains in income and wealth. What this account neglects, it is argued, is that "as people gain wealth, their formal freedoms become more valuable to them"—"increases in income" increase "the worth of the freedoms enjoyed by all citizens."[11]

The meaningful work account might overcome these objections, but the free time account is less vulnerable to such skepticism because free time is valuable in the same way as income and wealth are. As citizens gain more of the resource of free time, their formal freedoms are more valuable to them: they possess more of the means generally required to exercise their liberties. Citizens require both resources, but at some point of material development, the marginal value of more free time may be greater than the marginal value of more material wealth for the worth of their freedoms. As such, it may be the case that a society, once it has reached a certain level of wealth, could justly decide to forgo any further economic growth for the sake of guaranteeing more free time.

To summarize, to determine what constitutes a fair share of free time, there are four relevant considerations, the application of which will vary with the relevant theory of justice and empirical conditions: first, how much time a society must devote to the shared burdens of social cooperation, indicating the aggregate available amount of free time; second, which distributive principles apply to citizens' resource claims, whether egalitarian, sufficientarian, or another; third, the relative weights given to different resources, namely the values given to additional free time or material wealth; and fourth, whether any special intervening reasons apply to an individual's claim, such as an occupational choice which weakens one's pro tanto claim to free time.

11 John Tomasi, *Free Market Fairness* (Princeton: Princeton University Press, 2012), 190.

7.3 HOW? PUBLIC POLICY IMPLICATIONS

The preceding considerations indicate to how much free time citizens are entitled. A remaining question is, then, how citizens' claims are to be realized. Compared to citizens' claims to income and wealth, it is not as immediately apparent how it could be ensured that citizens have their fair shares of free time. While money can be directly redistributed, free time cannot simply be transferred from one bank account to another. Yet, though the state cannot directly redistribute free time, laws, regulations, and public provisions can, and do, significantly affect how much time it takes one to meet one's basic needs, to the effect that the state can, through a range of policy mechanisms, ensure that all citizens have their fair shares of free time.

Following the arguments of the preceding chapters, there are four essential features of citizens' claims to free time that must be met, insofar as it is possible to do so consistent with the other requirements of justice: if x is one's fair share of free time, one (1) must be able to meet one's basic needs in (24 – x) hours per day, and (2) must be able to choose to spend no more than (24 – x) hours per day meeting one's basic needs. Furthermore, (3) a sufficient portion of one's free time must be shared with one's current and potential associates, and (4) if one does not have discretion over when one's free time occurs, it must occur in generally usable periods and on a predictable schedule. There are a range of social arrangements that could realize these conditions, but here I will indicate some of the possible policy mechanisms that are most consonant with existing arrangements and feasible given them. For context, I will begin with a brief survey of the primary policies in the contemporary United States that directly relate to the distribution of free time.

Before proceeding to these policy mechanisms, it is important to note that citizens must have their fair shares of free time consistently over the life course. If citizens were to possess free time only during particular life stages—for instance, only after one's working years in retirement—that would be incompatible with the grounds of citizens' claims to free time. So long as one lacks free time, even with the promise of future free time, one lacks the means to enjoy the value of one's formal liberties and opportunities. Individuals might choose to spend their free time working during the primary years of their careers, but they must still have their fair shares of free time to spend as they so choose. While some periods of more and less free time, as with seasonal work, are still consistent with the effective freedoms principle, the periods must not be of too great duration.

Existing Time Policy in the United States

First, with respect to time engaged in paid work, the United States, compared to other developed countries, has relatively minimal regulations of work hours. There are no federal laws that specify the maximum number of hours that can be worked daily, weekly, or annually, the maximum number of days that can be worked per week, the times of the day that work can occur, or how much vacation time must be provided.[12] There are also no federal regulations that require employers to provide employees with short-hours work or flexible work schedules, nor that guarantee benefits or protections for employees who work part-time.[13]

The primary legislation that regulates working time is the Fair Labor Standards Act (FLSA), passed in 1938, which requires employers to pay covered employees premium wages for hours worked in excess of forty hours per week.[14] Apart from the provision for overtime pay, there is no upper limit on how many hours per day or per week an adult employee may work. The FLSA also places no restrictions on mandatory overtime; employers are permitted to require employees to work hours in excess of the standard workday and without advance notice.[15] In addition to providing covered employees relatively minimal restrictions and protections, many employees are exempt from the provisions of the FLSA—primarily professional, executive, managerial, and administrative workers paid on a salaried basis—to the effect that approximately one-quarter of all full-time employees are not covered.[16]

---

12 The few exceptions are for occupations in which long work hours could negatively affect the safety of others, as, for instance, with commercial motor vehicle drivers and aircraft flight crew members.

13 Ariane Hegewisch and Janet C. Gornick, "Statutory Routes to Workplace Flexibility in Cross-National Perspective" (Institute for Women's Policy Research and Center for Work-Life Law, 2007), 27–28.

14 Though individual states can supplement the FLSA with their own statutes, only a small number of states have additional overtime regulations.

15 Lonnie Golden and Helene Jorgensen, "Time after Time: Mandatory Overtime in the U.S. Economy" (Economic Policy Institute Briefing Paper, 2002).

16 The full list of exemptions also includes a wide array of occupational categories. Janet C. Gornick, Alexandra Heron, and Ross Eisenbrey, "The Work-Family Balance: An Analysis of European, Japanese, and U.S. Work-Time Policies" (Economic Policy Institute Briefing Paper 189, 2007), 3.

Second, with respect to time engaged in household and caregiving labor, the most significant policy is the Family and Medical Leave Act (FMLA), passed in 1993. The FMLA requires that all covered employers provide their employees with twelve weeks of unpaid leave, continuation of health insurance coverage, and reinstatement in the same or equivalent position to employees who request leave to care for themselves or their family members (specifically, for their own medical condition, including pregnancy, or to take care of a newborn child or newly adopted child, a parent, or a severely ill child or spouse). The FMLA does not entitle employees to leave to care for young children or other relations, nor does it entitle employees to reduced-hours work to provide caregiving. Moreover, only firms with more than fifty employees are covered by the FMLA, to the effect that over half of all employees are not eligible.[17]

Finally, with respect to time engaged in caring for one's own bodily needs, the only significant legislation beyond the FMLA, which applies to all workers with short-term illness or injuries, is the Americans with Disabilities Act (ADA), passed in 1990. The ADA applies to all citizens with a disability, defined as "a physical or mental impairment that substantially limits one or more of the major life activities," and requires employers (with fifteen or more employees) to provide reasonable accommodation to qualified employees, unless it would cause an undue burden on the operation of business. Reasonable accommodations include providing a disabled employee with a reduced-hours or flexible work schedule.[18]

Guaranteeing a Fair Amount of Free Time

For citizens to possess their fair share of free time, they must both have their fair *amount* of free time, and have it under fair *conditions* to make effective use of it. I focus first on the amount and then the conditions.

The claim to a fair share of free time, if x hours per day is the fair amount of free time, is in effect the claim to be able to spend no more than $(24 - x)$

17 Heidi Hartmann, Ariane Hegewisch, and Vicky Lovell, "An Economy That Puts Families First: Expanding the Social Contract to Include Family Care" (Economic Policy Institute Briefing Paper 190, 2007), 7.

18 Kathryn Moss and Scott Burris, "The Employment Discrimination Provisions of the Americans with Disabilities Act: Implementation and Impact," in *The Future of Disability in America*, ed. Marilyn J. Field and Alan M. Jette (Washington, DC: National Academies Press, 2007), 453–56; Richard V. Burkhauser and Mary C. Daly, "U.S. Disability Policy in a Changing Environment," *Journal of Economic Perspectives* 16 (2002): 213–24.

hours per day meeting one's basic needs. The aim is then to ensure that all citizens are able to spend no more than (24 − x) hours per day meeting their basic needs. This, again, entails two demands. First, it is necessary to ensure that all citizens can in fact *meet* their basic needs in (24 − x) hours per day. Second, it is necessary to ensure that all citizens can *choose* to spend no more than (24 − x) hours per day meeting their basic needs.

Accordingly, the types of justified policies fall into two categories. First, the claim to free time justifies policies that help citizens to meet their basic needs in less time so they can have their fair share. This means, broadly, income subsidies or in-kind provisions, and might include a universal basic income, minimum wage laws, income transfers or wage subsidies to low wage earners, targeted income subsidies to the temporarily and permanently disabled, targeted income subsidies to caregivers, and publicly provided caregiving services and facilities for the elderly, disabled, and children. Second, the claim to free time justifies regulations that protect citizens' ability to choose to spend no more time meeting their basic needs than is necessary to have their fair share. These regulations include maximum work hours provisions, restrictions on overtime work, and workplace accommodations for caregivers and the ill and disabled.

Before illustrating how these policies could be implemented to provide for free time, it is important to emphasize an unorthodox feature of these recommended labor regulations. In accordance with the justification for citizens' claims to free time, the ideal maximum hours regulation would serve two ends: (1) it would protect all employees' right to choose not to work longer hours than is necessary to meet their basic needs, and (2) it would allow employees to work longer hours than necessary if they choose. Citizens are entitled to free time to exercise the full range of their formal liberties and opportunities, to pursue their conceptions of the good, whatever they are, whether that means spending their free time involved in typically necessary activities—like additional paid work—or in conventional leisure activities. As such, the justification for guaranteeing citizens free time recommends labor regulations that allow citizens to use their free time for paid work.

However, if it is not possible to simultaneously achieve both ends, the regulations ought to cede the second condition to realize the first. In accordance with standard liberal egalitarian principles, providing the conditions for the effective exercise of the basic liberties, and thus free time, has priority over unfettered exercise of the economic liberties. This conflict arises if the desire of some employees to work longer hours undermines, through competitive pressures and social norms, the ability of other employees to choose not to work longer hours.

Maximum hours regulations that serve both ends could take different forms. Employees might, for instance, have a waivable right not to work hours above a maximum, with protections against retaliation if one chooses not to work more than the maximum hours.[19] Or there might be a general maximum hours limit with permission for some employees to opt out of the limit, perhaps with the condition that only a certain percentage of employees in a firm or occupation are permitted to opt out.[20] As an additional measure, overtime regulations could allow or require employees to take overtime compensation in the form of compensatory paid time off from work rather than additional wages.[21] If regulations of this sort proved ineffective in protecting all employees' right to choose not to work longer hours, then a prohibitive maximum hours regulation is justified, perhaps tailored to a particular industry or occupational category.[22]

To illustrate how these two sets of policies—income subsidies or in-kind provisions and labor regulations—could be implemented to provide for free time, I will give examples of individuals with deficiencies of free time resulting from the three realms of necessary activity, financial, household, and bodily. As will become clear, however, some types of policies could address free time deficiencies that arise in each realm. To fix the parameters for the sake of illustration, assume that citizens are entitled to a sufficient amount of free time, that citizens' claims to free time are conditional on their willingness to work, that caregiving for children and other dependents qualifies as necessary time, and that citizens are entitled to free time in their chosen occupational categories.

Say, more specifically, that citizens are entitled to fifty-six hours of free time per week, and that in a given society the typical amount of time that it

19 For a discussion of how to design such a waivable employee right so that it protects employees' rights both to choose to work longer hours *and* to choose not to, see Cass R. Sunstein, "Human Behavior and the Law of Work," *Virginia Law Review* 87 (2001): 205–76.

20 The United Kingdom, for instance, permits its citizens to opt out of the European Union's maximum hours regulation (of 48 hours per week).

21 Schor, *Overworked American*, 142–43.

22 A prohibitive maximum hours regulation would block employees from working longer than the maximum hours with a given employer, but would not necessarily block additional paid work undertaken with a second employer or independently, so long as this secondary employment would not produce the competitive pressures that undermine other citizens' ability to choose not to work longer hours.

takes one to meet one's bodily basic needs is seventy hours per week and to meet one's household basic needs ten hours per week, and that the standard level of basic financial need is twenty-five thousand dollars per year (without dependents). An individual with typical bodily and household basic needs must, then, be able to meet her financial basic needs with thirty-two hours of paid work per week in order to have her fair share of fifty-six hours per week of free time. Though this amount is only illustrative, it is not arbitrarily chosen, as it is the amount claimed in the labor slogan, "eight hours for what we will."

First, take A, who has typical household and bodily needs, but who must spend sixty hours per week engaged in paid work to meet her financial basic needs because she earns only eight dollars per hour. She accordingly has only twenty-eight hours of free time, half of her fair share. Two types of policies would redress her insufficiency of free time, wage subsidies or regulations and maximum hours laws. In order to ensure that A can meet her financial basic needs in only thirty-two hours per week, A requires some type of policy to augment her wage rate. Possible policies include income or wage subsidies, minimum wage laws, or both. Though necessary, these policies are not sufficient to guarantee her fair share of free time if she is unable to find employment in her occupation for only thirty-two hours per week. So, in addition, she must also be protected by a maximum hours regulation that guarantees her the right not to work more than thirty-two hours per week.[23]

Second, take B, who does thirty-two hours of paid work per week and who has typical bodily needs, but who spends fifty-six hours per week engaged in basic caregiving for his elderly parent and child. As such, he lacks any free time. Again, two types of policies would redress his deficiency of free time: first, public care provision and income subsidies and, second, short hours and caregiving leave regulations.[24]

23 To be clear, what a maximum hours law must protect is *not* the choice to work whatever hours one prefers, or the choice to work no more than is necessary to meet one's basic needs, but specifically the choice to work no more than is necessary to meet one's basic needs so that one has one's fair share of free time. If A earned $100 an hour, she would have to work less than five hours per week to meet her financial basic needs, but she is not entitled to work only five hours per week, for such an entitlement would guarantee her more than her fair share of free time. This point highlights a difference between my approach and Goodin et al.'s, which more generally recommends policies that "ensure that people have, insofar as possible, a free choice of the number of hours a week they work in paid labour" (*Discretionary Time*, 267; see also 102–5, 112).

24 I discuss both policy options from the perspective of B, assuming that B's parent has a sufficient amount of free time and is not, as such, entitled to any additional free time benefits. The policies could be designed, however, with B's parent as a beneficiary.

Public care provision, both for the elderly and children, would allow B to spend less time engaged in basic caregiving. Possibilities include, for the elderly (or disabled), full-time or part-time nursing homes, at-home nurse visits, delivered meals, or transportation services for the elderly, and for children, universal or means-tested access to public child care facilities, universal pre-kindergartens, and publicly provided before- and after-school care.[25] Income subsidies would also allow B to either spend less time in caregiving or less time in another necessary activity. He could use an income subsidy to hire someone to help care for his parent or child, to meet his own household needs, or to reduce his hours of paid work (or some combination of the three). By reducing the amount of time that B must spend in some combination of these three necessary activities, an income subsidy could allow B to meet his basic needs in the requisite amount of time.

Public provisions and income subsidies are, however, not sufficient to guarantee B his fair share of free time. To have the opportunity to engage in direct caregiving for his child, or if he objects to hiring someone to care for his parent or child (see 4.4), he must also be able to reduce his hours of paid work. As discussed in 6.5, a set of workplace accommodations for caregivers—periods of paid leave, extended short-hours schedules, and flexible or irregular work hours—would allow B to engage in caregiving and have his fair share of free time.[26] An additional institutional measure that could increase B's free time is to increase the synchronization between children's school schedules and parents' typical work schedules.[27]

Lastly, take C, who works thirty-two hours per week, but who has a disability that requires her to spend more time meeting her bodily and household needs than someone without a disability. Say it takes an additional thirty-two hours per week, so she has half of her fair share of free time. Again, in keeping with the two types of policies generally required to provide free time, both income subsidies and flexible work hours and disability leave regulations would guarantee her free time.

C's free time deficiency may seem to be a difficult one to redress, for it results in part from the time she must spend meeting her bodily basic needs,

---

25 See Hartmann, Hegewisch, and Lovell, "Economy That Puts Families First," 11–13.

26 For an overview of alternative work arrangements for caregivers in high-income countries, see Hegewisch and Gornick, "Statutory Routes to Workplace Flexibility in Cross-National Perspective," 14–18.

27 Joan C. Tronto, *Caring Democracy: Markets, Equality, and Justice* (New York: New York University Press, 2013), 166.

needs that only she can meet. Yet, because one's free time is the inverse of *all* the time one must spend meeting one's basic needs, whether household, financial, or bodily, it is possible for policies to target her deficiency of free time indirectly, by reducing the amount of time she must spend meeting her household or financial basic needs. Income subsidies would allow C either to hire someone to help meet her household needs or to reduce her hours of paid work. Such subsidies are again, however, not sufficient to ensure that C is guaranteed her fair share of free time, for she must also be able to reduce her hours of paid work. This requires, as for caregivers, access to short-hours employment or periods of employment leave.

Accordingly, short-hours regulations may be required to guarantee free time to both caregivers and the disabled. In both instances, short hours are required only for those who have additional caregiving or bodily basic needs. Short work hours, therefore, may justifiably be provided only to these eligible individuals. However, because universal provisions may be easier to implement and have lower administrative costs than those targeted to only eligible employees, it would also be justifiable to guarantee short hours to all employees.[28]

Guaranteeing Fair Conditions of Free Time

These two types of policies—income subsidies or in-kind provisions and work-hours regulations—can guarantee that citizens have the requisite amount of free time. But, citizens' shares of free time must also meet certain conditions. Consistent with the grounds of citizens' claims to free time, on the basis of the effective freedoms principle, citizens must generally be able to make effective use of their periods of free time to exercise their formal liberties and opportunities. Consider three examples, all of whom have in total fifty-six hours of free time per week: a live-in housekeeper and nanny whose free time is divided into fifteen minute periods because of the nature of her responsibilities; a factory worker whose free time does not occur on

---

28 Belgium, for instance, entitles all workers to a one-year sabbatical over the course of their working life, with the option of stretching the sabbatical over five years at 80 percent of one's normal hours. In Finland, in an effort both to provide reduced work hours and to address unemployment, all workers are entitled to part-time hours with partial wage replacement if an unemployed person is hired to replace their reduced hours. Hegewisch and Gornick, "Statutory Routes to Workplace Flexibility in Cross-National Perspective," 19–20.

a predictable schedule because he is regularly required to work overtime on short notice; and a retail employee whose free time occurs during weekdays because she is required to work weekends and evenings. Though such individuals do have the requisite amount of free time, they do not possess this time on conditions that allow them to effectively use it to exercise their liberties.

Two conditions must obtain. First, as I argued in Chapter 5, for effective freedom of association in particular, one must have reasonable access to sufficient periods of free time shared with a significant portion of those with whom one currently associates and might associate. This condition may be realized in a variety of ways, including by guaranteeing citizens abundant free time, work hours flexibility, or a common period of free time, as realized by Sunday free time laws.

Second, one must either have discretion over when one's free time occurs, or if one has limited discretion over the scheduling of one's free time, one's free time must occur in generally usable periods and on a predictable schedule. To take an example, in order to use one's free time to exercise one's political liberties, say by volunteering with a campaign for a shift knocking on doors and distributing pamphlets, one must possess a period of free time of sufficient duration to engage in this pursuit and one must be able to make plans and reliably commit to the shift. The greater the degree of discretion one has over when one's free time occurs, all else equal, the greater one's ability to make effective use of one's free time for the exercise of one's liberties. Though some citizens have a high degree of temporal autonomy, most citizens have limited discretion over when their free time occurs as a result of both internal and external constraints. Of particular importance for theories of justice, most citizens have limited discretion over when their free time occurs on account of their terms of employment, specifically their work schedules.

One way to meet this condition is to increase the degree of discretion employees have over their work schedules. Indeed, employee-initiated flexibility over work scheduling has increased to a significant extent over the past quarter century in developed economies. Insofar as this trend has made employees' free time more valuable to them, as it allows them greater opportunity to use their free time in pursuit of their chosen ends, it is to be welcomed. Increasing employees' discretion over when their free time occurs is, however, unlikely to be adequate. Individualized, flexible work schedules are economically costly to provide to many employees (given the costs of employment discussed in 4.4) and may be difficult if not impossible to provide to many more (given that some work must be done at certain times of the day and/or with co-workers). To some extent, to counteract these structural market features that favor uniform schedules, the state is justified in incentivizing employers to offer more employee-initiated flexibility in work schedules, but such incentives neither can do the impossible nor ought to be instituted at any cost.

Thus, for those employees who have limited discretion over their work schedules, their free time must occur in periods of sufficient duration and at predictable times. At the level of public policy, this condition requires that, for instance, employees be entitled to sufficiently long periods between work shifts and to regular or advance scheduling of work shifts. This condition also justifies restricting employers from requiring that employees be "on call" or responsive to work demands during their free time. As with maximum work hours, employees could have a waivable right not to work irregular or "always on" hours. Public policies could also require or incentivize employers to limit after-hours work communication. To the extent that unpredictable and on-call work schedules are necessary, as with work during common periods of free time, they could be shared on rotation.

To summarize, if x is the fair share of free time, insofar as it is possible to realize, one (1) must be able to meet one's basic needs in $(24 - x)$ hours per day, and (2) must be able to choose to spend no more than $(24 - x)$ hours per day meeting one's basic needs. Furthermore, (3) a sufficient portion of one's free time must be shared with one's current and potential associates, and (4) if one does not have discretion over when one's free time occurs, it must occur in generally usable periods and on a predictable schedule. A just society must meet these four parameters, and, as indicated here, there is a wide range of possible mechanisms to do so.

7.4 FREE TIME IN THE JUST SOCIETY

Depending on the choices citizens individually and collectively make, about both the weight to give free time and how to spend it, the patterns of time use in the just society may take a range of forms, from something recognizable to something only distantly imagined, like the stationary state welcomed by J. S. Mill, in which all are relieved from toil and can "cultivate freely the graces of life," or the futures seen by Bertrand Russell and J. M. Keynes in which all work only three or four hours a day.[29]

The essential feature is that in the just society all citizens would have their fair shares of free time. All citizens would have time not consumed by meeting the necessities of life, time that they could devote to their own pursuits and commitments, whatever those might be.

29 Mill, *Principles of Political Economy*, 124–30; Russell, "In Praise of Idleness," 1–15; John Maynard Keynes, "Economic Possibilities for Our Grandchildren," in *Essays in Persuasion* (1931); repr., New York: Norton, 1963), 358–73.

BIBLIOGRAPHY

Aguiar, Mark, and Erik Hurst. "Measuring Trends in Leisure: The Allocation of Time over Five Decades." *Quarterly Journal of Economics* 122 (2007): 969–1006.

Alesina, Alberto, Edward Glaeser, and Bruce Sacerdote. "Work and Leisure in the United States and Europe: Why So Different?" In *NBER Macroeconomics Annual 2005*, edited by Mark Gertler and Kenneth Rogoff, 1–64. Cambridge, MA: MIT Press, 2006.

Altonji, Joseph G., and Christina H. Paxson. "Labor Supply Preferences, Hours Constraints, and Hours-Wages Trade-offs." *Journal of Labor Economics* 6 (1988): 254–76.

Anderson, Elizabeth. "The Fundamental Disagreement between Luck Egalitarians and Relational Egalitarians." *Canadian Journal of Philosophy Supplementary Volume 36* (2010): 1–23.

———. "Justifying the Capabilities Approach to Justice." In *Measuring Justice: Primary Goods and Capabilities*, edited by Harry Brighouse and Ingrid Robeyns, 81–101. Cambridge: Cambridge University Press, 2010.

———. "Optional Freedoms." In *What's Wrong with a Free Lunch?*, edited by Joshua Cohen and Joel Rogers, 70–74. Boston: Beacon, 2001.

———. *Value in Ethics and Economics*. Cambridge, MA: Harvard University Press, 1993.

———. "What Is the Point of Equality?" *Ethics* 109 (1999): 287–337.

Aristotle. *Nicomachean Ethics*. Translated and edited by Terence Irwin. Indianapolis: Hackett, 1999.

———. *The Politics*. In *The Politics and Constitution of Athens*, edited by Stephen Everson, 11–207. Cambridge: Cambridge University Press, 1996.

Arneson, Richard J. "Equality and Equal Opportunity for Welfare." *Philosophical Studies* 56 (1989): 77–93.

———. "Equality of Opportunity for Welfare Defended and Recanted." *Journal of Political Philosophy* 7 (1999): 488–97.

———. "Feminism and Family Justice." *Public Affairs Quarterly* 11 (1997): 313–30.

———. "Meaningful Work and Market Socialism." *Ethics* 97 (1987): 517–45.

Arnold, Samuel. "The Difference Principle at Work." *Journal of Political Philosophy* 20 (2012): 94–118.

———. "Work as It Might Be: A Theory of Justice in Production." PhD dissertation, Princeton University, 2011.

Ås, Dagfinn. "Studies of Time-Use: Problems and Prospects." *Acta Sociologica* 21 (1978): 125–41.

Barry, Brian. "Spherical Justice and Global Injustice." In Miller and Walzer, *Pluralism, Justice, and Equality*, 67–80.

Başlevent, Cem, and Hasan Kirmanoğlu. "The Impact of Deviations from Desired Hours of Work on the Life Satisfaction of Employees." *Social Indicators Research* 118 (2014): 33–43.

Bedi, Sonu. *Rejecting Rights.* Cambridge: Cambridge University Press, 2009.

Beitz, Charles R. *The Idea of Human Rights.* Oxford: Oxford University Press, 2009.

Bell, David, Steffen Otterbach, and Alfonso Sousa-Poza. "Work Hours Constraints and Health." *Annals of Economics and Statistics* 105/106 (2012): 35–54.

Berlin, Isaiah. "Two Concepts of Liberty." In *Liberty*, edited by Henry Hardy, 166–217. 1958. Reprint, Oxford: Oxford University Press, 2002.

Bianchi, Suzanne M. "Family Change and Time Allocation in American Families." *Annals of the American Academy of Political and Social Science* 638 (2011): 21–44.

Birnbaum, Simon. "Should Surfers Be Ostracized? Basic Income, Liberal Neutrality, and the Work Ethos." *Philosophy, Politics & Economics* 10 (2011): 396–419.

Bittman, Michael. "Sunday Working and Family Time." *Labour & Industry* 16 (2005): 59–81.

Blau, Francine D., and Lawrence M. Kahn. "Female Labor Supply: Why Is the United States Falling Behind?" *American Economic Review* 103 (2013): 251–56.

———. "Gender Differences in Pay." *Journal of Economic Perspectives* 14 (2000): 75–99.

Borjas, George. *Labor Economics.* 7th ed. New York: McGraw-Hill, 2016.

Brady, Henry E., Sidney Verba, and Kay Lehman Schlozman. "Beyond SES: A Resource Model of Political Participation." *American Political Science Review* 89 (1995): 271–94.

Brighouse, Harry. "Neutrality, Publicity, and State Funding of the Arts." *Philosophy & Public Affairs* 24 (1995): 35–63.

Brighouse, Harry, and Adam Swift. "Equality, Priority, and Positional Goods." *Ethics* 116 (2006): 471–97.

———. "Parents' Rights and the Value of the Family." *Ethics* 117 (2006): 80–108.

Brown, D. G. "The Value of Time." *Ethics* 80 (1970): 173–84.

Buchanan, Allen. *Justice, Legitimacy, and Self-Determination: Moral Foundations for International Law.* Oxford: Oxford University Press, 2004.

———. "Revisability and Rational Choice." *Canadian Journal of Philosophy* 5 (1975): 395–408.

Bureau of Labor Statistics. "American Time Use Survey—2014 Results." News release. June 24, 2015.

———. "Employee Benefits in the United States—March 2015." News release. July 24, 2015.

———. "Unpaid Eldercare in the United States." News release. September 23, 2015.

Burkhauser, Richard V., and Mary C. Daly. "U.S. Disability Policy in a Changing Environment." *Journal of Economic Perspectives* 16 (2002): 213–24.

Burley, Justine, ed. *Dworkin and His Critics: with Replies by Dworkin.* Malden, MA: Blackwell, 2004.

Carens, Joseph H. *Equality, Moral Incentives, and the Market: An Essay in Utopian Politico-Economic Theory.* Chicago: University of Chicago Press, 1981.

Caruso, Claire C. "Possible Broad Impacts of Long Work Hours." *Industrial Health* 44 (2006): 531–36.

Casal, Paula, and Andrew Williams. "Rights, Equality and Procreation." *Analyse & Kritik* 17 (1995): 93–116.

Christofidis, Miriam Cohen. "Talent, Slavery, and Envy." In Burley, *Dworkin and His Critics*, 30–44.

Clarkberg, Marin, and Phyllis Moen. "Understanding the Time-Squeeze: Married Couples' Preferred and Actual Work-Hour Strategies." *American Behavioral Scientist* 44 (2001): 1115–36.

Cohen, G. A. "Freedom and Money." In Cohen, *On the Currency of Egalitarian Justice*, 166–92.

———. *Karl Marx's Theory of History: A Defence.* Expanded ed. 1978. Reprint, Princeton: Princeton University Press, 2000.

———. *On the Currency of Egalitarian Justice, and Other Essays in Political Philosophy.* Edited by Michael Otsuka. Princeton: Princeton University Press, 2011.

———. "On the Currency of Egalitarian Justice." In Cohen, *On the Currency of Egalitarian Justice,* 3–43.

———. *Rescuing Justice and Equality.* Cambridge, MA: Harvard University Press, 2008.

Contensou, François, and Radu Vranceanu. *Working Time: Theory and Policy Implications.* Cheltenham: Edward Elgar, 2000.

Cranston, Maurice. "Are There Any Human Rights?" *Daedalus* 112 (1983): 1–17.

———. "Human Rights, Real and Supposed." In *Political Theory and the Rights of Man,* edited by D. D. Raphael, 43–53. London: Macmillan, 1967.

———. *What Are Human Rights?* London: Bodley Head, 1973.

Daniels, Norman. "Democratic Equality: Rawls's Complex Egalitarianism." In Freeman, *Cambridge Companion to Rawls,* 241–76.

———. "Family Responsibility Initiatives and Justice Between Age Groups." *Law, Medicine and Health Care* 153 (1985): 153–59.

De Grazia, Sebastian. *Of Time, Work, and Leisure.* 1962. Reprint, New York: Vintage, 1994.

Dembe, Allard E. "Ethical Issues Relating to the Health Effects of Long Working Hours." *Journal of Business Ethics* 84 (2009): 195–208.

Depew, David J. "Politics, Music, and Contemplation in Aristotle's Ideal State." In *A Companion to Aristotle's Politics,* edited by David Keyt and Fred D. Miller, Jr., 346–80. Oxford: Blackwell, 1991.

Díaz, Antonia, and Cristina Echevarria. "Why a Fixed Workweek?" *Journal of Socio-Economics* 38 (2009): 790–98.

Dworkin, Ronald. *A Matter of Principle.* Cambridge, MA: Harvard University Press, 1985.

———. *Sovereign Virtue: The Theory and Practice of Equality.* Cambridge, MA: Harvard University Press, 2000.

Eichner, Maxine. *The Supportive State: Families, Government, and America's Political Ideals.* Oxford: Oxford University Press, 2010.

Fisher, Kimberly, Muriel Egerton, Jonathan I. Gershuny, and John P. Robinson. "Gender Convergence in the American Heritage Time Use Study (AHTUS)." *Social Indicators Research* 82 (2007): 1–33.

Fleurbaey, Marc. *Fairness, Responsibility, and Welfare.* Oxford: Oxford University Press, 2008.

Folbre, Nancy. "Children as Public Goods?" *American Economic Review* 84 (1994): 86–90.

———. *The Invisible Heart: Economics and Family Values.* New York: New Press, 2001.

———. *Valuing Children: Rethinking the Economics of the Family.* Cambridge, MA: Harvard University Press, 2008.

Foner, Philip S., ed. *We, the Other People.* Urbana: University of Illinois Press, 1976.

Foss, Clive. "Stalin's Topsy-Turvy Work Week." *History Today* 54 (2004): 46–47.

Franklin, Benjamin. *Franklin: The Autobiography and Other Writings on Politics, Economics and Virtue.* Edited by Alan Houston. Cambridge: Cambridge University Press, 2004.

Fraser, Nancy. "After the Family Wage: Gender Equity and the Welfare State." *Political Theory* 22 (1994): 591–618.

Freeman, Samuel, ed. *The Cambridge Companion to Rawls.* Cambridge: Cambridge University Press, 2003.

———. "Capitalism in the Classical and High Liberal Traditions." *Social Philosophy and Policy* 28 (2011): 19–55.

———. "Illiberal Libertarians: Why Libertarianism Is Not a Liberal View." *Philosophy & Public Affairs* 30 (2001): 105–51.

———. *Rawls.* New York: Routledge, 2007.

Genakos, Christos, and Svetoslav Danchev. "Evaluating the Impact of Sunday Trading Deregulation." Centre for Economic Performance Discussion Paper No. 1336, 2015.

George, Rolf. "On the External Benefits of Children." In *Kindred Matters: Rethinking the Philosophy of the Family*, edited by Diana Tietjens Meyers, Kenneth Kipnis, and Cornelius F. Murphy, Jr., 209–17. Ithaca: Cornell University Press, 1993.

———. "Who Should Bear the Cost of Children?" *Public Affairs Quarterly* 1 (1987): 1–42.

Gershuny, Jonathan. "Veblen in Reverse: Evidence from the Multinational Time-Use Archive." *Social Indicators Research* 93 (2009): 37–45.

Gheaus, Anca. "Gender Justice." *Journal of Ethics and Social Philosophy* 6 (2012): 1–24.

Gimenez-Nadal, Jose Ignacio, and Almudena Sevilla-Sanz. "The Time-Crunch Paradox." *Social Indicators Research* 102 (2011): 181–96.

Golden, Lonnie. "A Brief History of Long Work Time and the Contemporary Sources of Overwork." *Journal of Business Ethics* 84 (2009): 217–27.

———. "The Economics of Worktime Length, Adjustment, and Flexibility: A Synthesis of Contributions from Competing Models of the Labor Market." *Review of Social Economy* 54 (1996): 1–45.

Golden, Lonnie, and Tesfayi Gebreselassie. "Overemployment Mismatches: The Preference for Fewer Hours of Work." *Monthly Labor Review* 130 (2007): 18–37.

Golden, Lonnie, and Helene Jorgensen. "Time after Time: Mandatory Overtime in the U.S. Economy." Economic Policy Institute Briefing Paper 120, 2002.

Golden, Lonnie, and Barbara Wiens-Tuers. "Mandatory Overtime Work in the United States: Who, Where, What?" *Labor Studies Journal* 30 (2005): 1–26.

Goodin, Robert E., James Mahmud Rice, Michael Bittman, and Peter Saunders. "The Time-Pressure Illusion: Discretionary Time vs. Free Time." *Social Indicators Research* 73 (2005): 43–70.

Goodin, Robert E., James Mahmud Rice, Antti Parpo, and Lina Eriksson. *Discretionary Time: A New Measure of Freedom*. Cambridge: Cambridge University Press, 2008.

Gornick, Janet C., Alexandra Heron, and Ross Eisenbrey. "The Work-Family Balance: An Analysis of European, Japanese, and U.S. Work-Time Policies." Economic Policy Institute Briefing Paper 189, 2007.

Gourevitch, Alex. *From Slavery to the Cooperative Commonwealth: Labor and Republican Liberty in the Nineteenth Century*. New York: Cambridge University Press, 2015.

Griffin, James. *On Human Rights*. Oxford: Oxford University Press, 2008.

Gutmann, Amy. "Justice Across the Spheres." In Miller and Walzer, *Pluralism, Justice, and Equality*, 99–119.

Hamermesh, Daniel S. "Changing Inequality in Work Injuries and Work Timing." *Monthly Labor Review* 122 (1999): 22–30.

Hamermesh, Daniel S., and Elena Stancanelli. "Long Workweeks and Strange Hours." *ILR Review* 68 (2015): 1007–18.

Hart, H.L.A. "Are There Any Natural Rights?" *Philosophical Review* 64 (1955): 175–91.

Hart, Robert A. *The Economics of Overtime Working*. Cambridge: Cambridge University Press, 2004.

Hartmann, Heidi, Ariane Hegewisch, and Vicky Lovell. "An Economy That

Puts Families First: Expanding the Social Contract to Include Family Care." Economic Policy Institute Briefing Paper 190, 2007.

Hegewisch, Ariane, and Janet C. Gornick. "Statutory Routes to Workplace Flexibility in Cross-National Perspective." Institute for Women's Policy Research and Center for WorkLife Law, 2007.

Hochschild, Arlie Russell. *The Second Shift.* New York: Avon Books, 1989.

———. *The Time Bind: When Work Becomes Home and Home Becomes Work.* New York: Metropolitan Books, 1997.

Hook, Sidney. *Philosophy and Public Policy.* Carbondale: Southern Illinois University Press, 1980.

Hsieh, Nien-Hê. "Justice in Production." *Journal of Political Philosophy* 16 (2008): 72–100.

Hunnicutt, Benjamin Kline. *Free Time: The Forgotten American Dream.* Philadelphia: Temple University Press, 2013.

Jacobs, Jerry A., and Kathleen Gerson. *The Time Divide: Work, Family, and Gender Inequality.* Cambridge, MA: Harvard University Press, 2004.

Kahneman, Daniel, and Alan B. Krueger. "Developments in the Measurement of Subjective Well-Being." *Journal of Economic Perspectives* 20 (2006): 3–24.

Keynes, John Maynard. "Economic Possibilities for Our Grandchildren." In *Essays in Persuasion*, 358–73. 1931. Reprint, New York: Norton, 1963.

Klagge, James C. "Marx's Realms of 'Freedom' and 'Necessity.'" *Canadian Journal of Philosophy* 16 (1986): 769–77.

Kleiner, Sibyl, and Eliza K. Pavalko. "Clocking In: The Organization of Work Time and Health in the United States." *Social Forces* 88 (2010): 1463–86.

Klosko, George. *Political Obligations.* Oxford: Oxford University Press, 2005.

Kraut, Richard. *Aristotle: Political Philosophy.* Oxford: Oxford University Press, 2002.

Krueger, Alan B., Daniel Kahneman, David Schkade, Norbert Schwarz, and Arthur A. Stone. "National Time Accounting: The Currency of Life." In *Measuring the Subjective Well-Being of Nations: National Accounts of Time Use and Well-Being*, edited by Alan B. Krueger, 9–86. Chicago: University of Chicago Press, 2009.

Laband, David N., and Deborah Hendry Heinbuch. *Blue Laws: The History, Economics, and Politics of Sunday Closing Laws.* Lexington, MA: Lexington Books, 1987.

Lahart, Justin, and Emmeline Zhao. "What Would You Do with an Extra Hour? Americans Are Spending More Time Watching TV and Sleeping as Unemployment Rises, Survey Finds." *Wall Street Journal*, eastern ed., June 23, 2010.

Landefeld, J. Steven, Barbara M. Fraumeni, and Cindy M. Vojtech. "Accounting for Household Production: A Prototype Satellite Account Using the American Time Use Survey." *Review of Income and Wealth* 55 (2009): 205–25.

Landers, Renée M., James B. Rebitzer, and Lowell J. Taylor. "Rat Race Redux: Adverse Selection in the Determination of Work Hours in Law Firms." *American Economic Review* 86 (1996): 329–48.

Larmore, Charles. "The Idea of a Life Plan." *Social Philosophy and Policy* 16 (1999): 96–112.

Lawrence-Hammer, Lesley. "Red, White, but Mostly Blue: The Validity of Modern Sunday Closing Laws Under the Establishment Clause." *Vanderbilt Law Review* 60 (2007): 1273–1306.

Lee, Sangheon, Deirdre McCann, and Jon C. Messenger. *Working Time around the World: Trends in Working Hours, Laws, and Policies in a Global Comparative Perspective.* New York: Routledge, 2007.

Lord, Carnes. *Education and Culture in the Political Thought of Aristotle.* Ithaca: Cornell University Press, 1982.

Macedo, Stephen, et al. *Democracy at Risk: How Political Choices Undermine Civic Participation, and What We Can Do About It.* Washington, DC: Brookings Institution Press, 2005.

Mankiw, N. Gregory. *Principles of Economics.* 7th ed. Stamford, CT: Cengage Learning, 2015.

Martinez-Granado, Maite. "Testing Labour Supply and Hours Constraints." *Labour Economics* 12 (2005): 321–43.

Marx, Karl. *Karl Marx: Selected Writings.* Edited by David McLellan. 2nd ed. Oxford: Oxford University Press, 2000.

Mattingly, Marybeth J., and Suzanne M. Bianchi. "Gender Differences in the Quantity and Quality of Free Time: The U.S. Experience." *Social Forces* 81 (2003): 999–1030.

McClain, Linda C. *The Place of Families: Fostering Capacity, Equality, and Responsibility.* Cambridge, MA: Harvard University Press, 2006.

McCrossen, Alexis. *Holy Day, Holiday: The American Sunday.* Ithaca: Cornell University Press, 2000.

McGowan v. Maryland, 366 U.S. 420. (1961).

Menefee, John Alsworth. "The Economics of Leisure: The Evolution of the Labor-Leisure Tradeoff in Economic Doctrines." PhD dissertation, Duke University, 1974.

Messenger, Jon C. "Towards Decent Working Time." In *Decent Working Time: New Trends, New Issues*, edited by Jean-Yves Boulin, Michel Lallement, Jon C. Messenger, and François Michon, 419–41. Geneva: International Labour Office, 2006.

Milkie, Melissa A., Sara B. Raley, and Suzanne M. Bianchi. "Taking on the Second Shift: Time Allocations and Time Pressures of U.S. Parents with Preschoolers." *Social Forces* 88 (2009): 487–518.

Mill, J. S. *On Liberty and Other Essays*. Edited by John Gray. Oxford: Oxford University Press, 1991.

———. *Principles of Political Economy and Chapters on Socialism*. Edited by Jonathan Riley. Oxford: Oxford University Press, 1994.

Miller, David. *Principles of Social Justice*. Cambridge, MA: Harvard University Press, 1999.

Miller, David, and Michael Walzer, eds. *Pluralism, Justice, and Equality*. Oxford: Oxford University Press, 1995.

Moss, Kathryn, and Scott Burris. "The Employment Discrimination Provisions of the Americans with Disabilities Act: Implementation and Impact." In *The Future of Disability in America*, edited by Marilyn J. Field and Alan M. Jette, 453–77. Washington, DC: National Academies Press, 2007.

Muirhead, Russell. *Just Work*. Cambridge, MA: Harvard University Press, 2004.

Murphy, James Bernard. *The Moral Economy of Labor: Aristotelian Themes in Economic Theory*. New Haven: Yale University Press, 1993.

Musgrave, R. A. "Maximin, Uncertainty, and the Leisure Trade-Off." *Quarterly Journal of Economics* 88 (1974): 625–32.

Nussbaum, Martha C. *Women and Human Development: The Capabilities Approach*. Cambridge: Cambridge University Press, 2000.

Okin, Susan Moller. *Justice, Gender, and the Family*. New York: Basic Books, 1989.

Olsaretti, Serena. "Children as Public Goods?" *Philosophy & Public Affairs* 41 (2013): 226–58.

———. *Liberty, Desert, and the Market: A Philosophical Study*. Cambridge: Cambridge University Press, 2004.

Olson, Kristi A. "Leisure." In *The Cambridge Rawls Lexicon*, edited by Jon Mandle and David A. Reidy, 433–34. Cambridge: Cambridge University Press, 2015.

———. "Our Choices, Our Wage Gap?" *Philosophical Topics* 40 (2012): 45–61.

O'Neill, Martin. "What Should Egalitarians Believe?" *Philosophy & Public Affairs* 36 (2008): 119–56.

Otsuka, Michael. "Liberty, Equality, Envy, and Abstraction." In Burley, *Dworkin and His Critics*, 70–78.

Owens, Joseph. "Aristotle on Leisure." *Canadian Journal of Philosophy* 11 (1981): 713–23.

Parfit, Derek. "Equality or Priority?" In *The Ideal of Equality*, edited by Michael Clayton and Andrew Williams, 81–125. London: Macmillan, 2000.

Patten, Alan. "Are the Economic Liberties Basic?" *Critical Review* 26 (2014): 362–74.

———. "Liberal Neutrality: A Reinterpretation and Defense." *Journal of Political Philosophy* 20 (2011): 249–72.

Pettit, Philip. *On the People's Terms: A Republican Theory and Model of Democracy.* Cambridge: Cambridge University Press, 2012.

———. *Republicanism: A Theory of Freedom and Government.* Oxford: Oxford University Press, 1997.

Phillips, Anne. "Defending Equality of Outcome." *Journal of Political Philosophy* 12 (2004): 1–19.

Pieper, Josef. *Leisure, the Basis of Culture.* Translated by Alexander Dru. New York: Pantheon Books, 1952.

Pogge, Thomas W. *Realizing Rawls.* Ithaca: Cornell University Press, 1989.

Pope, Clayne. "Measuring the Distribution of Material Well-Being: U.S. Trends." *Journal of Monetary Economics* 56 (2009): 66–78.

Presser, Harriet B. "Employment Schedules among Dual-Earner Spouses and the Division of Household Labor by Gender." *American Sociological Review* 59 (1994): 348–64.

———. *Working in a 24/7 Economy: Challenges for American Families.* New York: Russell Sage, 2003.

Price, Jamie, and Bruce Yandle. "Labor Markets and Sunday Closing Laws." *Journal of Labor Research* 8 (1987): 407–14.

Putnam, Robert D. *Bowling Alone: The Collapse and Revival of American Community.* New York: Simon & Schuster, 2000.

Quong, Jonathan. *Liberalism without Perfection.* Oxford: Oxford University Press, 2010.

Radin, Margaret Jane. *Contested Commodities.* Cambridge, MA: Harvard University Press, 1996.

Rakoff, Todd D. *A Time for Every Purpose: Law and the Balance of Life.* Cambridge, MA: Harvard University Press, 2002.

Rakowski, Eric. *Equal Justice.* Oxford: Clarendon Press, 1991.

Rawls, John. "The Idea of Public Reason Revisited." In Rawls, *Law of Peoples*, 131–80.

———. *Justice as Fairness: A Restatement*. Edited by Erin Kelly. Cambridge, MA: Belknap, 2001.

———. *The Law of Peoples*. Cambridge, MA: Harvard University Press, 1999.

———. *Political Liberalism*. New York: Columbia University Press, 1993.

———. "The Priority of Right and Ideas of the Good." *Philosophy & Public Affairs* 17 (1988): 251–76.

———. "The Priority of Right and Ideas of the Good." In Rawls, *Political Liberalism*, 173–211.

———. "Reply to Alexander and Musgrave." *Quarterly Journal of Economics* 88 (1974): 633–55.

———. "Social Unity and Primary Goods." In *John Rawls: Collected Papers*, edited by Samuel Freeman, 359–87. Cambridge, MA: Harvard University Press, 1999.

———. *A Theory of Justice*. Original ed. Cambridge, MA: Belknap, 1971.

———. *A Theory of Justice*. Revised ed. Cambridge, MA: Belknap, 1999.

Ray, Rebecca, Milla Sanes, and John Schmitt. "No-Vacation Nation Revisited." Center for Economic and Policy Research, 2013.

Raz, Joseph. *The Morality of Freedom*. Oxford: Clarendon Press, 1986.

Rebitzer, James B., and Lowell J. Taylor. "Do Labor Markets Provide Enough Short Hour Jobs? An Analysis of Work Hours and Work Incentives." *Economic Inquiry* 33 (1995): 257–73.

Reich, Rob. *Bridging Liberalism and Multiculturalism in American Education*. Chicago: University of Chicago Press, 2002.

Reynolds, Jeremy. "In the Face of Conflict: Work-Life Conflict and Desired Work Hour Adjustments." *Journal of Marriage and Family* 67 (2005): 1313–31.

———. "You Can't Always Get the Hours You Want: Mismatches between Actual and Preferred Work Hours in the U.S." *Social Forces* 81 (2003): 1171–99.

Reynolds, Jeremy, and Lydia Aletraris. "Pursuing Preferences: The Creation and Resolution of Work Hour Mismatches." *American Sociological Review* 71 (2006): 618–38.

Richards, David L., and Benjamin C. Carbonetti. "Worth What We Decide: A Defense of the Right to Leisure." *International Journal of Human Rights* 17 (2013): 329–49.

Risse, Mathias. *On Global Justice*. Princeton: Princeton University Press, 2012.

———. "A Right to Work? A Right to Leisure? Labor Rights as Human Rights." *Law & Ethics of Human Rights* 3 (2009): 1–39.

Risse, Mathias, and Robert C. Hockett. "Primary Goods Revisited: The 'Political Problem' and Its Rawlsian Solution." Cornell Law Faculty Publications, Paper 55, 2006.

Robinson, John P., and Geoffrey Godbey. *Time for Life: The Surprising Ways Americans Use Their Time.* 2nd ed. University Park: Pennsylvania State University Press, 1999.

Rodríguez, Ariel, Pavlína Látková, and Ya-Yen Sun. "The Relationship between Leisure and Life Satisfaction: Application of Activity and Need Theory." *Social Indicators Research* 86 (2008): 163–75.

Roediger, David R., and Philip S. Foner. *Our Own Time: A History of American Labor and the Working Day.* London: Verso, 1989.

Rosenzweig, Roy. *Eight Hours for What We Will: Workers and Leisure in an Industrial City, 1870–1920.* Cambridge: Cambridge University Press, 1983.

Russell, Bertrand. "In Praise of Idleness." In *In Praise of Idleness: And Other Essays*, 1–15. 1935. Reprint, Abingdon: Routledge, 2004.

Rybczynski, Witold. *Waiting for the Weekend.* New York: Penguin, 1991.

Sandel, Michael. *What Money Can't Buy: The Moral Limits of Markets.* New York: Farrar, Straus and Giroux, 2012.

Satz, Debra. *Why Some Things Should Not Be for Sale: The Moral Limits of Markets.* Oxford: Oxford University Press, 2010.

Scanlon, T. M. *The Difficulty of Tolerance: Essays in Political Philosophy.* Cambridge: Cambridge University Press, 2003.

———. "The Diversity of Objections to Inequality." In Scanlon, *Difficulty of Tolerance*, 202–18.

———. "Preferences and Urgency." In Scanlon, *Difficulty of Tolerance*, 70–83.

———. "Rawls' Theory of Justice." *University of Pennsylvania Law Review* 121 (1973): 1020–69.

———. *What We Owe to Each Other.* Cambridge, MA: Belknap, 2000.

Scheffler, Samuel. "Choice, Circumstance, and the Value of Equality." *Philosophy, Politics & Economics* 4 (2005): 5–28.

———. *Death and the Afterlife.* Edited by Niko Kolodny. Oxford: Oxford University Press, 2013.

———. "What Is Egalitarianism?" *Philosophy & Public Affairs* 31 (2003): 5–39.

Schor, Juliet B. *The Overworked American: The Unexpected Decline of Leisure.* New York: Basic Books, 1992.

Schulte, Brigid. *Overwhelmed: How to Work, Love, and Play When No One Has the Time.* New York: Farrar, Straus, and Giroux, 2014.

Schwartz, Adina. "Meaningful Work." *Ethics* 92 (1982): 634–46.

———. "Moral Neutrality and Primary Goods." *Ethics* 83 (1973): 294–307.

Sen, Amartya. "Poor, Relatively Speaking." *Oxford Economic Papers* 35 (1983): 153–69.

Sharp, Clifford. *The Economics of Time.* New York: Wiley, 1981.

Shields, Liam. "The Prospects for Sufficientarianism." *Utilitas* 24 (2012): 101–17.

Shiffrin, Seana Valentine. "Paternalism, Unconscionability Doctrine, and Accommodation." *Philosophy & Public Affairs* 29 (2000): 205–50.

Shippen, Nichole Marie. *Decolonizing Time: Work, Leisure, and Freedom.* New York: Palgrave Macmillan, 2014.

Skidelsky, Robert, and Edward Skidelsky. *How Much Is Enough? Money and the Good Life.* New York: Other Press, 2012.

Smith, Adam. *An Inquiry into the Nature and Causes of the Wealth of Nations.* 1776. Reprint, Oxford: Oxford University Press, 1976.

Smith, Tom W. "A Cross-National Comparison on Attitudes towards Work by Age and Labor Force Status." Organisation for Economic Co-operation and Development, December 2000.

Solmsen, Friedrich. "Leisure and Play in Aristotle's Ideal State." *Rheinisches Museum für Philologie* 107 (1964): 193–220.

Sousa-Poza, Alfonso, and Alexandre Ziegler. "Asymmetric Information about Workers' Productivity as a Cause for Inefficient Long Working Hours." *Labour Economics* 10 (2003): 727–47.

Sparks, Kate, Cary Cooper, Yitzhak Fried, and Arie Shirom. "The Effects of Hours of Work on Health: A Meta-analytic Review." *Journal of Occupational and Organizational Psychology* 70 (1997): 391–408.

Stanczyk, Lucas. "Productive Justice." *Philosophy & Public Affairs* 40 (2012): 144–64.

Sunstein, Cass R. "Human Behavior and the Law of Work." *Virginia Law Review* 87 (2001): 205–76.

Swaine, Lucas A. "Principled Separation: Liberal Governance and Religious Free Exercise." *Journal of Church and State* 38 (1996): 595–619.

Sylvis, William. *The Life, Speeches, Labors and Essays of William H. Sylvis.* Edited by James C. Sylvis. 1872. Reprint, New York: Augustus M. Kelley, 1968.

Teitelman, Michael. "The Limits of Individualism." *Journal of Philosophy* 69 (1972): 545–56.

Tobin, James. "On Limiting the Domain of Inequality." *Journal of Law and Economics* 13 (1970): 263–77.

Tomasi, John. *Free Market Fairness*. Princeton: Princeton University Press, 2012.

Tronto, Joan C. *Caring Democracy: Markets, Equality, and Justice*. New York: New York University Press, 2013.

———. "The 'Nanny' Question in Feminism." *Hypatia* 17 (2002): 34–51.

Van Parijs, Philippe. "Difference Principles." In Freeman, *Cambridge Companion to Rawls*, 200–240.

———. "Equality of Resources versus Undominated Diversity." In Burley, *Dworkin and His Critics*, 45–69.

———. *Real Freedom for All: What (if Anything) Can Justify Capitalism?* Oxford: Oxford University Press, 1995.

———. "Why Surfers Should Be Fed: The Liberal Case for an Unconditional Basic Income." *Philosophy & Public Affairs* 20 (1991): 101–31.

Veblen, Thorstein. *The Theory of the Leisure Class*. 1899. Reprint, New York: Penguin, 1979.

Verba, Sidney, Kay Lehman Schlozman, and Henry E. Brady. *Voice and Equality: Civic Voluntarism in American Politics*. Cambridge, MA: Harvard University Press, 1995.

Vespa, Jonathan, Jamie M. Lewis, and Rose M. Kreider. "America's Families and Living Arrangements: 2012." Current Population Reports, P20-570. Washington, DC: U.S. Census Bureau, 2013.

von Platz, Jeppe, and John Tomasi. "Liberalism and Economic Liberty." In *The Cambridge Companion to Liberalism*, edited by Steven Wall, 261–81. Cambridge: Cambridge University Press, 2015.

Waldron, Jeremy. *Liberal Rights: Collected Papers, 1981–1991*. Cambridge: Cambridge University Press, 1993.

———. "Money and Complex Equality." In Miller and Walzer, *Pluralism, Justice, and Equality*, 144–70.

Walzer, Michael. *Spheres of Justice: A Defense of Pluralism and Equality*. New York: Basic Books, 1983.

Weeks, Kathi. *The Problem with Work: Feminism, Marxism, Antiwork Politics, and Postwork Imaginaries*. Durham, NC: Duke University Press, 2011.

Wellman, Carl. *The Proliferation of Rights: Moral Progress or Empty Rhetoric*. Boulder, CO: Westview, 1999.

White, Stuart. *The Civic Minimum: On the Rights and Obligations of Economic Citizenship*. Oxford: Oxford University Press, 2003.

————. "The Egalitarian Earnings Subsidy Scheme." *British Journal of Political Science* 29 (1999): 601–22.

Williams, Andrew. "Incentives, Inequality, and Publicity." *Philosophy & Public Affairs* 27 (1998): 225–47.

Williams, Joan. *Unbending Gender: Why Work and Family Conflict and What to Do about It.* Oxford: Oxford University Press, 2000.

Winship, Christopher. "Time and Scheduling." In *The Oxford Handbook of Analytical Sociology*, edited by Peter Hedström and Peter Bearman, 489–520. Oxford: Oxford University Press, 2009.

Young, Cristobal, and Chaeyoon Lim. "Time as a Network Good: Evidence from Unemployment and the Standard Workweek." *Sociological Science* 1 (2014): 10–27.

Zerubavel, Eviatar. *The Seven Day Circle: The History and Meaning of the Week.* 1985. Reprint, Chicago: University of Chicago Press, 1989.

INDEX

Americans with Disabilities Act (ADA), 137
Anderson, Elizabeth, 71, 122n18
anti-paternalism, 7–8, 27–29, 30, 34, 36
Aristotle, 31–32, 37
Arneson, Richard, 26n15, 114n4
arts, state support for, 8, 29, 34n33

basic liberties, 70, 74, 107–8, 138
basic needs, 42–45; basic needs approach to
    determining how much time is required
    for necessary activities, 54–55, 60–61; and
    deficiencies of free time, 139–42; defined,
    42n5, 58; and disabilities, 141–42; free
    time defined as time not engaged in meet-
    ing basic needs of self and dependents,
    37–40, 42, 45–50, 58–60; and individual
    responsibility, 60–61; and minimum aggre-
    gate amount of free time in a given society,
    128, 129, 134; and perfect substitutability
    of money and basic needs satisfaction, 77,
    81–84; and Rawls's primary goods, 45n8;
    and social benchmark approach, 53–56;
    and society's obligations, 62, 119–20, 123–
    24, 128–29; and Sunday closing laws, 110;
    and time-affecting circumstances, 47n14;
    and time-targeted provisions of distrib-
    utive justice theories, 89–90; typically nec-
    essary activities, 42, 48–50, 53–54, 58 (*see
    also* children and childcare; employ-
    ment; household responsibilities; per-
    sonal care)
Berlin, Isaiah, 70, 70n5
Bittman, Michael, 98n9
Blackstone, William, 103n15
Blau, Francine D., 116n7
Blue laws. *See* Sunday closing laws
Braunfeld v. Brown, 103n14

Brighouse, Harry, 125n25
Buchanan, Allen, 22
burdens of social cooperation, shared, 20–21,
    85, 128, 129, 134. *See also* basic needs: and
    society's obligations

capabilities theory, 25–26n15, 33, 33–34n32
caregiving, 5–6, 112–26; Family and Medical
    Leave Act, 137; and free choice among
    just background conditions, 117–19, 124;
    gender and free choice among equal
    options, 114–16; and imperfect substi-
    tutability of money and basic needs satis-
    faction, 81, 83–84; and individual
    responsibility, 62–64; and just back-
    ground conditions for household re-
    sponsibilities, 119–23, 126; public care
    provisions, 140–41; and society's obliga-
    tions, 62, 72n12, 119–20, 123; statistics
    on, 11–12; and Sunday closing laws, 110;
    as typically necessary activity, 48 (*see
    also under* children and childcare); and
    work-family balance, 124–26; workplace
    accommodations for parents and care-
    givers, 6, 69, 112–14, 124–26, 138, 140–42.
    See also children and childcare; gender;
    household responsibilities
children and childcare: childcare as nec-
    essary activity, 72–73, 90, 112, 114, 119–
    23, 139; children as "socialized goods"
    (Olsaretti's conception), 122n17; chil-
    dren's claims to free time, 63n29; choice
    to have children, 63–64, 72, 120, 123; and
    conceptions of the good, 44–45, 121–22;
    and gender justice, 113–14; parenting
    as providing a public good, 113, 120–
    23; public care provisions, 140, 141; and